D1496856

RITES OF DEATH AND DYING

Three Papers Given at the 1987 National Meeting
of the Federation of Diocesan Liturgical Commissions

Lawrence Boadt, C.S.P.
Mary Dombeck
H. Richard Rutherford, C.S.C.

Editor: Anthony F. Sherman

THE LITURGICAL PRESS
Collegeville, Minnesota

THE LITURGICAL PRESS
Collegeville, Minnesota 56321

Cover design by MARY JO PAULY

Copyright © 1988 by The Order of St. Benedict, Inc., Collegeville, Minnesota.
All rights reserved. Printed in the United States of America.

9	8	7	6	5	4	3	2	1

Library of Congress Cataloging-in-Publication Data
Federation of Diocesan Liturgical Commissions.
  National Meeting (20th : 1987 : Breckenridge, Colo.)
  Rites of death and dying.
    1. Funeral service—Congresses. 2. Unction—
Congresses. 3. Viaticum—Congresses. 4. Catholic
Church—Liturgy—Congresses. I. Boadt, Lawrence.
II. Dombeck, Mary. III. Rutherford, H. Richard.
IV. Sherman, Anthony F. V. Title.
BX2015.8.R4F43 1987   265'.85   88-8349
ISBN 0-8146-1597-X

Contents

Foreword

At one time or another we all face the experience of losing someone whom we love. The adjustment to this loss is challenging, and more than ever before the Church is attempting to respond to that challenge with sensitive and healing pastoral care.

It is no surprise then that at the twentieth annual meeting of the Federation of Diocesan Liturgical Commissions held at Breckenridge, Colorado, in 1987 the theme was the rites of death and dying. The insights and reflections offered by three of the main speakers at that gathering are now printed here for all who are helping others face the mystery of death.

Fr. Lawrence Boadt, C.S.P., sets the scene for the dialogue between death and dying and the Scriptures with the image of "going alone into the alone." Describing the elements of grief exemplified in the experience of C. S. Lewis, he then turns to the Scriptures in search for an understanding of this mystery of life. Exploring the psalms of lament highlights the contribution they can make in handling grief. Finally, he studies and positively critiques the use of Scripture in our present funeral rites.

From an anthropological perspective, the question of death rituals and American values is addressed by Mary Dombeck. In a study illustrated with abundant life examples, she explores three questions: (1) Do we find uniformity in funerary customs and death rituals in a society which historically and actually contains such ethnic diversity? (2) If there is uniformity in the midst of diversity, what might funerary customs and death rituals tell us about life values in this society? (3) Finally, how do the customs and rituals transform the fact of spiritual death into social, religious, and spiritual reality for the participants?

Looking closely at the empirical evidence available, Fr. H. Richard Rutherford, C.S.C., exercises an empirical, hermeneutical, and critical analysis of the funeral liturgy to answer a very specific question. Using standard social science methods he gropes with a precisely defined issue: Does the funeral liturgy function in a meaningful way in the bereavement experience of religious Catholics (specifically widowed persons, who as a group constitute a manageable population as well as one at high risk)? Some of Rutherford's conclusions give encouragement and support to those engaged in ministry to the bereaved. As plurality of belief and expression increases, however, it will be most essential for the Church and its ministers to be even more present, consoling, and supportive to those who are grieving.

The authors are indeed successful in getting us to look at the North American Christian cultural scene as it relates to death and dying. What is even more valuable, however, is that we are led to face the question of exactly how effective the presentation of liturgical symbols in the rites of death and dying are in communicating the Paschal Mystery as a hope-filled balm to those in grief. Finally, we also begin to get a glimpse of what factors might be at work within the average North American Christian that prevents the hope-filled message of Jesus Christ from penetrating.

ANTHONY F. SHERMAN
BROOKLYN DIOCESAN LITURGICAL COMMISSION
BROOKLYN, NEW YORK

The Scriptures on Death and Dying and the New Funeral Rite

LAWRENCE BOADT, C.S.P.

In his book *A Grief Observed*, C. S. Lewis tells how his wife, dying from cancer, would often quote to him the proverb, "Alone into the alone."[1]

This struck Lewis deeply and made the grief he experienced at the separation caused by her death all the more acute. He tried to picture her just as she had been so that he would not lose her presence. But when he gradually emerged from his grief to rediscover other people in his life, he found that this recovered awareness of the world actually sharpened his memory of his wife and made her more alive and part of his existence than all his maudlin efforts had been able to do in the midst of his denial of her death. She had not gone alone, nor was he alone without her.

Lewis' insight into his own personal sorrow explains one major purpose of formal church liturgy at the death of a person. It directly addresses the question of going alone into the alone. Christian conviction insists that we do not forget Christ's presence to us in the moment of death. Jesus declares, "It is the will of him who sent me that I should lose nothing of what he has given me, rather that I should raise it up on the last day" (John 6:39), or "'My sheep hear my voice; I know them and they follow me. I give them eternal life and they shall never perish" (John 10:27-28). In declaring the power of the death and resurrection of Jesus for all believers, living and dead, Paul tells the Thessalonians, "We would have you be clear about those who sleep in death, brothers; otherwise, you might yield to grief, like those who have no hope" (1 Thess 4:13). In the same way the Book of Revelation envisions the death of the martyrs: "The lamb on the throne shall shepherd them. He will lead them to springs of life-giving water, and God will wipe away every tear from their eyes" (Rev 7:17).

But a death is also part of the life of the community. Paul's treatment of what happens to those who have died in 1 Thessalonians and 1 Corinthians 15 highlights the unity of the living Church with those who have died, and the great hymn of Colossians 1:15-20 describes the cosmic rule of Christ, who is "the first-born of the dead," over living and dead alike. Paul also emphasizes both Christ's presence to and the union of all other disciples with the deceased when he declares, "While we live we are responsible to the Lord, and when we die, we die as his servants. Both in life and death, we are the Lord's. That is why Christ died and rose again, that he might be Lord of both the dead and the living" (Rom 14:8-9).

C. S. Lewis' book offers a second powerful statement in the opening sentence: "No one told me that grief felt so like fear. I am not afraid, but the sensation is like being afraid."[2] Here, Lewis focuses on the mourners and their sense of grief. The great writer seems to echo the words of the psalmists, who speak of their fear before enemies and sickness and misfortune: "My heart has become like wax melting away in my bosom" (Ps 22:15). "Do not fear the terror of the night nor the arrow that flies by day nor the pestilence that roams in darkness" (Ps 91:5-6). Against this fear the psalmists can declare: "Even though I walk in the valley of death, I fear no evil" (Ps 23:4), and "The Lord is my light and my salvation, whom should I fear?" (Ps 27:1). Here confidence in God dispels fear. And this, too, then, is a reason for the funeral liturgy: to help channel grief into hope.

David Dempsey, in his book *The Way We Die*, has summarized a number of studies that show prolonged bereavement can lead to mental disorders and psychosomatic diseases.[3] It certainly falls to the funeral liturgy—from the moment of the news of the death of a person on through the series of possible rites and memorials—to help channel that bereavement process into a healthy movement from the devastating effects of loss to healing and then to hope for the deceased in the life to come. Finally, the mourners reenter a positive and realistic place in the world without the deceased—but not without a healthy memory of the lost one.

Loneliness, fear, and other aspects of the bereavement process need the liturgy to help channel their potentially negative energy into a realization of a shared community of faith in tragedy and a trust in the God of life. Only in the liturgical rites are the three aspects brought together fully, i.e., the deceased individual with his or her grieving loved ones, the community, and God. All three must be part of the bereavement process for a true healing and reintegration to take place.

One of the most profound of Lewis' insights comes at the end of his grieving process, after he has filled four notebooks with his lamentations and mourning, and it is finally about God.

The notes, he says, that he has written, have been about

himself, his wife, and God, in that order. But the order and proportions are exactly the opposite of what they ought to have been. He nowhere fell into the mode of praising God, or really even his wife, and that would have been the best for him. Praise, he notes, is the mode of love which always has some element of joy in it.[4] Praise given in due order would first recognize God as the generous giver, his wife as the gift, and himself as the beneficiary.

THE ROLE OF THE SCRIPTURES

In noting the elements of grief above which one man has experienced, I answered them with references to passages of the Bible that offer both a reflection of that grief and a proclamation of hope. This is the most natural thing in the world for a Jew or Christian to do because we consider the Scriptures as a normative guide to the understanding of the ultimately religious mysteries of life. The Bible shapes our own self-identity as religious people who ask the meaning of events beyond our comprehension. The very scope of the biblical story and the breadth of its literary reflections on the different aspects of our human life provide the opportunity to discover the proper relationship among ourselves as individuals and as community within our relationship to God.

The General Instruction to the *Order of Christian Funerals* selects five reasons for reading God's Word: (1) to proclaim the paschal mystery, (2) to teach remembrance of the dead, (3) to convey the hope of being gathered again into God's kingdom, (4) to encourage the witness of Christian life, and (5) to tell of God's designs for a world in which suffering and death will relinquish their hold on all whom

God has called his own.[5] These are broadly conceived goals
that cover the whole range from affirming the kerygma of
the Scriptures down to practical help for the bereaved to
hold on to the memory of their beloved one and to regroup
their lives. In proclaiming the kerygma of God's salvation
in the Old Testament, and the mystery of Christ's passion,
death, and resurrection in the New, the reading of Scripture is directed as much to the rest of the community as
to those who have been personally touched by the death
of the beloved.

Yet, today, even with the advent of a revised *Order of
Christian Funerals,* several recent commentators have
pointed to even more that Scripture can offer in the liturgical celebration of the funeral rites, especially in the area of
recognizing and accepting the pain, loss, seeming irrational-
ity and meaninglessness of death that every mourner like
C. S. Lewis must pass through before claiming as his or her
own the message of hope and victory over death found in
those same Scriptures.

Thus I would like to review several aspects of the biblical view of death itself by sketching some of the information we know about ancient Israel's customs surrounding
death, by mentioning some theological attitudes towards
death found in the Scriptures, and, finally, by discussing some
of the recent suggestions about the value of the lament
psalms for broadening our own understanding of the
bereavement process.

THE HEBREW SCRIPTURES ON THE NATURE OF DEATH

The conception of death in the Hebrew Scriptures is not
delineated like a clear set of laws from the Torah, but rather

like a jigsaw puzzle in which we have many pieces, but not all that will be needed to understand the design completely. Part of this is due, no doubt, to the nature of the Scriptures themselves, which are concerned to proclaim the power of God over life and which do not focus on the enduring results of failure and death. Another part is due to the curious anomaly that biblical literature, alone among all ancient religious writings, avoids almost entirely any mention of the afterlife until very late in pre-Christian times. This contrasts strongly to the preoccupation with caring for the dead, built on the correlation between a proper interment and the hope for an afterlife, that dominated Egyptian, Mesopotamian, and Canaanite (Ugaritic) literature.[6]

The Bible prescribes no mandated way of conducting a funeral liturgy. Several practices associated with the death of an individual are described, but they rarely reveal the inner understanding of Israel on the question of what death really means in terms of continued life.[7] At the news of a death, mourners would pour dust or ashes on their heads (Josh 7:6; 1 Sam 1:12; Lam 2:10; Job 2:12), a practice also prescribed for penitential rites; tear their garments (Job 1:20; Josh 7:6; 2 Sam 1:11; 3:31; Gen 37:34); put on sackcloth (Gen 38:34; Isa 58:5); sit in silence on the ground (Num 11:4; Deut 1:45; Job 2:12; Lam 2:10); and avoid contact with the body to prevent uncleanness (Num 5:2; 19:1-22; Lev 21:1-12). Texts also provide us with a number of specific rites to be carried out. Spices were burned at funerals, at least of high officials (Jer 34:5; 2 Chr 16:14; 21:19); weeping and lamentations were performed by professional dirge singers (Ezek 32:16; 2 Chr 35:25; Ezek 27:32); fasting was required for a period of time (Esther 4:1-3); and it was usual to let one's hair grow long and not be cut (Ezek 44:20). There may have

been a funeral feast, a *marzeah*, which was commonly prac-
ticed among the Canaanites but less certainly in Israel;
apparent allusions exist in Amos 6:7; Jer 16:4-7; Ezek
24:16-17. References also occur in some of these passages
to a "bread of mourners" that was eaten.[8]

Some customs were widespread but officially condemned, such as shaving the head or beard (recorded in Isa
22:12; Job 1:20; Jer 7:29; 16:6; 41:5; 48:37; Ezek 7:18; Amos
8:10; but condemned by Lev 19:27-28). Gashing the body
was also well known in Ugaritic documents but forbidden
in Israel, probably because of its importance in pagan cul-
tic rites (Lev 19:24; cf. Jer 16:16).

Bodies were to be buried, and not cremated (2 Sam 25),
except for serious crime (Josh 7). Proper burial was important, but any further contact with the dead was repeatedly
condemned in Israel. The most notorious example is the attempt of King Saul to contact the ghost of the prophet
Samuel before the battle of Mount Gilboa in 1 Samuel 28.
Although the story treats necromancy as really possible, the
authors condemn the practice outright and consider it the
final sin of Saul that seals his coming death which Samuel
had earlier prophesied. Necromancy is also condemned in
Leviticus 20:6, 27; Deuteronomy 18:9, 11; Isaiah 8:19.

One biblical usage in which we have extensive confirmation from other ancient literature is that of metaphors
and names for death. Sheol is called "The Hidden Place"
(Job 40:13), the "Plain" (Ps 31:9), the "Mire" (Job 17:2),
the "Pit" (Isa 14:19), the "Ruin" (Ps 73:18), the "House"
(Isa 14:18), the "Place of Silence" (Ps 94:17; 115:17),
"Destruction" (Prov 15:11), "Perdition" (Ps 73:18), "Deep
Darkness" (Job 10:21; Ps 49:20), the "Slippery Place" (Ps
66:9), "The Land of Dust" (Job 34:15), "The City" (Ps 9:15),

"The Place of Ceasing" (Ps 17:11). Death is personified as "Sir Death" (Isa 25:6f), "The Ravenous One" (Ps 33:19), "The Enemy" (Ps 13:3), "The King of Terror" (Job 18:14), and "The Swallower" (*Belial*) (Ps 18:6).[9]

A further source of information is the intricate geography of the nether world described by both Isaiah 14 and Ezekiel 32. Both are in the context of a polemic against foreign kings. The prophets use the mythopoetic descriptions common in Akkadian and Ugaritic literature, especially in the epilogue to the Gilgamesh Epic (Tablet XII).[10] The dead are grouped by nations into separate areas where they lie without movement but can perceive new arrivals to the land of the dead. They are pictured as bitter and scornful, but with different states according to their ranks in life. Kings have thrones (Isa 14:9), while those who died ignobly or unburied have little but maggots for a cover (Isa 14:11). In Ezekiel 32:16-32, ancient heroes are buried and lie with honor, while the hated Assyrians and their allies lie scorned. Both Isaiah and Ezekiel picture Sheol as a land of weakness, silence and inert bodies.

This view of death is largely supported by the few other references we possess, especially from the Psalms. Psalm 94:17 refers to the underworld as "The land of Silence" (cf. Ps 49:12-13); Psalm 6:6 laments that no one can praise God from the underworld (cf. also Pss 30:10; 88:11; 115:17; Isa 28:18-19; 38:11; Qoh 9:5-6; Sir 17:27). In a similar manner, the earlier books of the Bible describe an ordinary death as "to sleep with one's fathers" (Gen 47:40; Deut 31:16; 1 Kgs 11:21), or "to be gathered to one's ancestors" (Gen 25:8, 17; 35:29; 49:29; Judg 2:10; 2 Kgs 22:20). This suggests that the dead will be remembered honorably but will be inactive. A note of fear about death is often present. A person may be swallowed by Sheol (Isa 25:8) or caught in the ropes of death and brought down (Ps 18:6). In this and similar references to the use of nets to ensnare a person, death is conceived as a fowler hunting birds (Qoh 7:26; Job 18:8-10; Ps 42:7).[11]

In general, the view throughout all but the last period of Old Testament history was that humans will return to the dust from which they came (Gen 3:19), without power or possessions (Ps 49:17; Job 15:29-30), without memory, joy, or voice to praise God. Qoheleth, the consummate sceptic, sums it up perfectly: "Give and take, indulge yourself, for in Sheol there will be no happiness" (14:16).

SOME THEOLOGICAL REFLECTIONS ON DEATH IN THE HEBREW SCRIPTURES

The first and most important theological conclusion about death in the major part of Old Testament thought is that it is so final. The spirit leaves this life for good (Ps 104:29; Job 34:14-15; Qoh 12:7). So the limits of all action and all hope are kept within the bounds of this life. When Psalms 16:9; 49:16; or 73:23-25 declare that the psalmist trusts life fully to Yahweh, the message contains both the hope for a long life now and a faith that God controls the quality of life now and checks the power of death. Israel may then experience the goodwill and favor of God rather than the divine anger or the unleashing of the power of evil in the world.

In this way of thinking, the ideal death came after fullness of years, i.e., after a long life (Gen 25:8, 15; Job 5:26; 21:23-24; 29:18-20). One left behind many children to be remembered by (Job 5:25; Isa 53:10) and departed this world quickly and painlessly (Job 21:13-15). A bad death is the opposite: it is premature. Hezekiah laments, "In the noontime of my days, I must depart; my home is plucked up and taken from me like a shepherd's tent" (Isa 38:10, 12). It is childless (Gen 15:2-3; 2 Sam 18:18; Sir 44:9), and it is often violent (Ezek 32:16-32; 1 Sam 15:32; 1 Kgs 2:28-33).

One hope that all could cling to was that the just person who obeyed the law of God would live on in the memory of the assembly that worshipped Yahweh. Isa 56:3-5 promises the eunuch, though childless, that he will receive in the temple, "a monument and a name better than sons or daughters; an eternal, imperishable name will I give them." Sirach 44:1-15 recalls the lives of great ancestors and those whose names are forgotten but who are remembered for piety by the worshipping assembly (cf. also Prov 10:7).

In fact, ancient Israel was much less anxious about the question of immortality or life after death than any of its neighbors. It understood death to be from within the natural course of life as God determined it, while its pagan neighbors feared death as an enemy from without. They often personified death as a divine power or god in its own right who challenged the ability of the gods of order to protect life against its attack. This is the essence of the Baal cycle of myths in the Ugaritic documents.

Israel, on the other hand, related the power of life and death to God alone so that both were under one guiding hand. God had the power to prolong life or to shorten it for reasons unknown to us (1 Kgs 19:4; 1 Sam 2:6-7; Job 1:21; 34:14-15). Both the individual and the nation were subject to the plan of God which was inscrutable to human searchings (Isa 40:12-26; Job 28). Thus emphasis fell more on the quality of life for the people as a whole according to God's commands than on the hope for the survival of individuals.

Mesopotamian religion had long been preoccupied with the afterlife, even if it was not much more of an existence for the majority of dead than Israel itself had pictured for its Sheol. Israel resisted this preoccupation with life after death, for reasons that are not altogether clear—many scholars suggest it was in reaction to the emphasis that an ever-repeating cycle of life and death received in pagan systems.[12] But, in fact, the monotheistic faith of Israel had a life-bias. It stressed an enduring covenant between God and the people, a primacy of ethical behavior with clear distinctions between the good and the wicked, and an understanding of time and history which always moved toward God's future.

Thus it was natural that the hope should arise that the future would be better and that the communion established with God by the covenant bonds would not be broken by the power of death (Ps 73; Job 14:13-14). On one level, prophetic eschatology developed a theology of a remnant by which God would preserve the unending life of the people as a whole, but which would not prevent the deaths of individuals. On another level, the ancient myth of Yahweh's victory over the forces of chaos was now concretized as the hope of Yahweh's victory over the power of death for the individual. Imagery such as the resurrection of the dead bones to life in Ezekiel 37 added fuel to this hope. Wisdom reflections on the deserved fates of the good and the wicked led also to an expectation that the good would be rewarded in the Day of the Lord to come (cf. Zech 8:1-8; Isa 24:21-23; possibly also Job 19:25-27). Apocalyptic thinking grew from both prophecy and wisdom and envisioned the dramatic end to this world and its life in favor of a world to come. The first appearance of an explicit hope in afterlife in the Bible comes in Daniel 12:1-3 from the early second century before Christ, but it was well prepared for by these internal developments of hope in God's unbroken commitment to Israel. Mention of resurrection of the dead occurs repeatedly after this: in 1 Enoch, 4 Ezra, the Book of Wisdom and the Books of Maccabees; and of course, in the New Testament, and later in the Rabbinic writings of the Talmud.[13]

The New Testament

Up to this point I have not mentioned the attitudes of the New Testament towards death and dying. On a biological level, physical descriptions and specific customs at the time of death do not differ markedly from those in the Hebrew Scriptures, except that in burials, after the flesh has decayed, the bones were gathered into small ossuaries so that the body would be all in one place on the day of the resurrection.[14] But on the theological level, the New Testament places the question of life and death to the fore of its reflection. The question of life after death is crucial to the interpretation of Jesus' death and resurrection for St. Paul in 1 Corinthians 15 and in 1 Thessalonians 4-5. Death cannot be part of God's original plan for the world because it is a result of human sinfulness at the beginning of creation according to Romans 5:18-19, 6:23, 8:19-22. Even the Gospel stories of Jesus' death picture the fearfulness of this power of death that seems to conquer all (Mark 14:33-37; 15:34; cf. Heb 5:7).

The authoritative interpretation of Jesus' death and resurrection is the claim that God has defeated the power of death (Rom 8:19-20; 1 Cor 15:25-26; Eph 6:12), and broken its power over us, both in this life and the life to come (Rom 8:21-22; Matt 10:28-29; Rev 20:10, 14) so all can hope for resurrection and life to come (1 Cor 15:12, 20; Rev 21:3-4).

St. John constantly affirms the eternal nature of life in Christ already (John 1:4; 3:36; 5:24; 10:17-18;12:23-24). The landscape of such reflections embodies the developments found in the later Hebrew Scriptures: different fates in heaven and hell for the good and the wicked, the possibility of resurrection on the apocalyptic day, and belief in the power of an evil angelic force of sin and death.[15]

One striking difference between the general description of death as an event for the individual in the Hebrew Scriptures and in the New Testament is that for the bulk of Israelite reflection life after the grave has little or no bearing on action in this life. In the New Testament, on the other hand, implications for present attitudes and behavior are rife. Stories of Jesus' concern to raise the dead found in the Gospels (Luke 7:11-17; 8:40-56; John 11:18-44), and the close connection between accepting the death and resurrection of Jesus and becoming a disciple (Mark 8:31-38; Acts 2:29-39), as well as Paul's profound reflections on dying and rising with Christ (Rom 5-8; 2 Cor 4), all connect who and what we are now with what we shall become in the life after death.

The New Testament may seem to concentrate much more on the anxiety of the individual over death and afterlife than does the Old Testament, but, in reality, death and life in the New Testament are always associated with the present communal dimensions of the Body of Christ, discipleship, and living in Christ (1 Cor 12:12-26; Rom 8:24-34; Gal 2:20). The later New Testament writings stress the connection between the quality of life now and the hope of life to come. The First Letter of Timothy sums this up when it says: "Fight the good fight of faith, take hold firmly on the everlasting life to which you were called when you made

your noble profession of faith before so many witnesses"
(1 Tim 6:12); and a little later it adds, "Charge them to do
good, to be rich in good works and generous, sharing what
they have. Thus they will build a secure foundation for the
future, for receiving that life which is life indeed" (1 Tim
6:18-19).

THE POWER OF THE LAMENT PSALM

In a recent article Richard Rutherford and Robert Sparkes
have evaluated the role of the funeral liturgy within the
bereavement process.[16] In this, they use insights drawn from
studies of the lament psalms by Claus Westermann and
Walter Brueggemann[17] to highlight that there are parts to
the form of the lament psalm that correspond to the three
major stages in bereavement: separation, liminality, and reintegration of the mourners into the community and back
to ordinary life. Their study is an excellent example of how
biblical teaching can be applied to the findings of modern
social sciences and to contemporary liturgical expression.

Westermann's great insight was to show that the Psalter could be classified in only two basic forms: that of praise
and that of lament. The lament itself always has many dimensions: it has elements directed towards God, towards others
and towards self (the same insight that C. S. Lewis came
to on his own!); it can be made not only for the dead, but
for the living in deadly crisis; and it looks both backwards
to loss and forward to help and healing. But ultimately, even
the lament must be seen within the intention of the psalmists
to offer praise to God. There is an unbreakable connection
between lament and praise so that although raging at God
and pleading with God are both permitted, it can only be
done inside the context of praising the goodness of God.[18]

Brueggemann has written several articles to enlarge on the dialectic aspects of Westermann's insights. He applies the paradigm of the Exodus event as the model for Israel's prayer of lament: oppression, cry for help, answer and deliverance. And since not only the experience of slavery in Egypt, but the period in the wilderness, the threat of conquest by the Philistines, the inroads of the Baal cult under the kings, the Assyrian and Babylonian invasions, and the Exile are all patterned after the Exodus event, the entire religious stance of the Bible is conceived according to this lament model. In our common human frailty, the people of the covenant community call on God, expect an answer, and experience the healing, saving, and liberating power of God in our lives. Ultimately, then, the loneliness of death or of bereavement must be taken up in the patterns we have learned from (a) our own experience as part of the weak and sinful *community at prayer* and (b) the proclamation of the acts and promises of God heard from others and believed by us within the community.

Brueggemann uses such contrasting concepts as uncreation and recreation, disorientation and reorientation, unreason and reason.[19] In mediating the movement from one to the other, the community plays an essential role, especially in liturgy, by articulating both the lament, the petition, the past experience of the nation, and the certitude of trust by means of the familiar and consecrated language of well-honed forms of prayer. For both individual and people, the pain of disorientation and unreason are sandwiched within a consciousness that begins with an acknowledgement of divine order (i.e., of creation, orientation, and reason) and moves to healing through the recognition that one can be reinserted into God's overall good purpose by responding to the divine offer of compassion (i.e., recreation, reorientation, return to reason).

Scholars have identified many of the settings of lament psalms in specific liturgical settings in Israel, such as trials for those falsely accused (Pss 7, 26, 27) or penitential rites (Pss 38, 39, 51). Perhaps the most famous is the so-called *Heilsorakel*, or healing oracle over the sick person. Several psalms move dramatically from a complaint about illness or desolation to praise of the God who has heard. In between these two parts, there is either a short word of Yahweh or simply a rhythmic break where perhaps a prophet or priest would say a blessing over the psalmist-sufferer. Examples occur in Psalms 6, 12, 22, 60, 91 and 108 among others.[20] Although this idea presupposes the cry of an individual for help, what is striking is how similar this pattern is to national prayers for help found in communal psalms of lament such as Psalms 60, 74, 79, 83 or 89. An instructive example is the passage in 2 Chronicles 20 where king Jehoshaphat is being hard pressed by a combined attack of Moabites and Ammonites and summons all the people to Jerusalem to pray. They gather as one, fast, and pray in common. Then the king stands up and prays on behalf of all the people that God will not forget what he has done for them in the past nor his promise to stand by them when the people come *to his temple* in distress.

Suddenly, a prophet stands up and delivers the word of God: do not fear! God will deliver you in the battle. Immediately after this the king and people bow down to the ground together in humble worship and then stand and sing hymns of praise to God for the victory *not yet* in their hands.

Interestingly enough, this liturgical prayer of lament uses many of the customs associated with funeral rites and periods of mourning. Another detailed story of national lament occurs in Nehemiah 9 in which the leader asks the people to cover their heads with ashes, wear sackcloth and fast while praying and asking divine forgiveness. This is followed by the reading of Scripture, humble bowing down in worship, an act of submission to God's will, and a blessing of God's name. Similar scenes are mentioned in Joel 1:13-14 and 1 Maccabees 3:47, which also includes reading of the Scriptures.

These observations on various aspects of the lament tradition in the Scriptures remind us how closely the concerns of the individual in a time of tragic loss are identified with the public suffering and past experience of the community. This is the point where liturgy enters the picture as mediator between the grief of the individual and the ability of the community to absorb that grief and transform it to hope within the community's ongoing trust in, and reliance on, the promises of the God who has spoken in its midst words of salvation and deliverance.

Rutherford and Sparkes have focussed mostly on the usefulness of the lament to help take seriously the pain of loss and separation and articulate it with the bereaved, so that they can properly hear the word of hope in the liturgy. I would simply add a few further observations to their insight. First, we all know, and the lament psalm reinforces our conviction, that no liturgical rites are adequate unless they bring together the individual sufferer, the God who saves, and the rest of the community. Second, the psalms of lament remind us that grief is handled in the context of prayer from beginning to end. Israel never offered a complaint list to God by itself. It is a dialogue with God in prayer, and above all, in praise.

Third, I like a proposal of Jay Goldingay that Israel's laments are a *circle* of praise. They do not move merely from disaster to pleading to answer, but go back and forth and are repeated in every life situation in a kind of spiral, so that each journey around finds us in a new place with a new perspective.[21]

Fourth, all the lament psalms are part of the Psalter and must be read together with the hymns of praise and thanksgiving. Above all, the Psalter is headed by Psalm 1 which clearly understands that those who say these psalms "delight in the law of the Lord and meditate on that law day and night." The psalms are not our words to God any longer but a response to God's prior word to us. The psalms have become God's word of promise to us, and the strong messianic hope in the current order of the Psalter is intended to be read also with the psalms of lament.[22]

Fifth, I like the insight of John Craghan that the psalms of lament are a school of prayer in which we must face life head on and not deny its difficulties, but let go of our fear to look beyond ourselves to a generous God. But at the same time, by asking help in a troubled world, we open ourselves to the demands of God's world of concern and are implicitly committed to offering help to other people. He says, "To cry out for help means to be willing to hear the community's cry for help."[23]

Finally, the New Testament reflects the same understanding when people cry out to Jesus and he answers them (Mark 5:7; Matt 9:27; 14:30; 15:23; etc.). Jesus himself prays the prayer of lament and opens himself to the larger world of God's life-giving power through his death and resurrection; and he invites his disciples to join him. Indeed, the psalms have always been the favorite Christian prayer because they resonate so completely with the New Testament pattern of salvation.

REFLECTIONS ON THE NEW RITE OF FUNERALS

I have steered clear of any detailed treatment of how the biblical teaching on death and dying conforms to modern studies of the bereavement process because so much has already been written on this topic. I have tried to underscore the importance of the liturgical setting of Old Testament passages on coping with death and tragedy because only in the communion of the individual with the community of faith does an integrating healing take place. The Bible, both Old and New Testaments, understood this well, and the chief challenge that needs to be laid before the Christian community today is to absorb and know the Scriptures better. Their stories of divine deliverance largely remain lifeless for most people except as the promise of life after death found in the Gospels. The dramatic and sensitive treatments of real life pain, prayer and divine response, found throughout the Bible, are not known.

I applaud the studies that point out how the new funeral liturgy emphasizes the threefold dimension of the individual, the community, and God interacting in the grieving process. I also agree with the observations that even the revised *Order of Christian Funerals* provides too few biblical texts that come to grips with the absurdity and meaninglessness of death. Texts and prayers alike leap a little too quickly to the proclamation of hope and life.[24]

On the other hand I am impressed with several features of the new revision that enhance the biblical input into the funeral liturgy. There is added weight given in the general instruction to the role of the scriptural readings and psalms (#22–27),[25] as well as in the particular instructions for individual rites, such as the vigil (#59–61) or the funeral Mass liturgy (#137–141). There is the addition of the Office of the Dead with its emphasis on the psalms that can be now readily used by all involved in funeral planning. There is a series of prayers for the placing of symbols on the coffin which give a good explanation and, for example, encourage us to actually put the book of the Gospels on it (#400). There are new prayers which are much more biblical in language and imagery and so are distinct improvements over earlier prayers from the 1971 book (examples include #282B, #398, #404, #404c). And finally, there are new rites for important moments in the grieving process before the actual funeral liturgy itself. These include the Prayers after Death (#101–108); Gathering in the Presence of the Body (#109–118); and the Transfer of the Body to the Church or Place of Committal (#119–127). These new opportunities do broaden the moments when the ministers of the Church can comfort the family and insert more recognition of feelings of loss, pain, and senselessness at the time of death. They correspond to the stage of separation in the bereavement process and to the first part of the lament psalm as paradigm for our human situation in which we express our need before turning to God.

These new additions and improvements in the revised *Order of Christian Funerals* provide a more holistic context of the Church's ministry in the time of death. It invites the ministers and community members to be more actively present in the grieving process outside of just attending a wake and funeral Mass.

Some final suggestions might be made, such as the need

for more reading of the Bible by those who study liturgy so that the lessons of Scripture can be better incorporated into liturgical texts; the development of more Old Testament texts that express the hard reality of loss and grief for sharing with the bereaved in early stages of preparing for the funeral liturgy; and more work on the homily as a means of expressing both the wrenching loss and the great hope that we Christians acknowledge. The homily should also avoid making too great a separation between the dead and the living by reaffirming the communion of saints celebrated in our rites.[26]

On the other hand, the liturgy cannot be expected to do everything for the moment of loss, for the process of coming to accept the loss, or for reintegration into ordinary life again. The funeral liturgy does what all liturgy does best: it proclaims anew the kerygma of God's salvation, compassion, presence, and life in moments when we are likely to forget it or need to hear it the most. It turns our thoughts, especially in deep grief, away from feeling sorry for ourselves and from being utterly alone and towards the praise of God, where we will rediscover the right place of the deceased, ourselves, and the community—all under God's rule of life. It denies C.S. Lewis' fear of going alone into the alone; it allows us all to share the journey he made from that devastating aloneness to new meaning in life through the discovery of praise: God first, as the giver; the deceased second, as the gift; and ourselves third, as the ones blessed.

NOTES

1. C. S. Lewis, *A Grief Observed* (New York: Seabury Press, 1961) 15.
2. *Ibid.* 7.
3. David Dempsey, *The Way We Die* (New York: Macmillan, 1975) chapter 7.
4. Lewis, *A Grief Observed* 49. See also his more developed reflections on praise in Christian life in his *Reflections on the Psalms* (New York: Harcourt Brace, 1958) 93-98.
5. *Order of Christian Funerals* (Washington: International Commission on English in the Liturgy, 1985) #22.
6. Lloyd Bailey, Sr., *Biblical Perspectives on Death* (Philadelphia: Fortress Press, 1979) 5-22, "Some Perspectives on Death among Israel's Neighbors."
7. See standard dictionaries of the Bible for details; e.g., John L. McKenzie, *Dictionary of the Bible* (Milwaukee: Bruce Publishing Co., 1965) 183-85.
8. For further details on the funeral feast, see Marvin Pope, *Song of Songs* (Anchor Bible 7C; Garden City, N.Y.: Doubleday, 1977) 214-29.
9. These are all documented in Nicholas Tromp, *Primitive Conceptions of Death and the Netherworld in the Old Testament* (BibetOr 21; Rome: Pontifical Biblical Institute, 1969) 168-72, 187-90.
10. See James Pritchard, *Ancient Near Eastern Texts Relating to the Old Testament* 3rd ed. (Princeton: Princeton University Press, 1969) 97-99.
11. See Tromp, *Primitive Conceptions* 172-75.
12. Mircea Eliade, *Cosmos and History* (New York: Harper & Row, 1959) 1-48.
13. See O. S. Rankin, *Israel's Wisdom Literature: Its Bearing on Theology and the History of Religion* (Edinburgh: T. & T. Clark, 1936) 124-221. Clear speculation about immortality, perhaps under the influence of Greek ideas, appears in Wis 3:3-4; 5:15-16; 8:13; 2 Macc 7:9-36; 4 Macc 14:5; 16:13, 25; 17:12; 18:3, 23.
14. See L. Rahmani, "Ancient Jerusalem's Funerary Customs and Tombs," *Biblical Archaeologist* 44(1981) 171-78.
15. See Wis 2:23-24; 2 Macc 7:10-11; and the treatment in Bailey, *Biblical Perspectives on Death* 75-86.
16. Robert Sparkes and Richard Rutherford, "The Order of Christian Funerals: A Study in Bereavement and Lament," *Worship* 60(1986) 499-510.

17. Claus Westermann, *Praise and Lament in the Psalms* (Atlanta: John Knox, 1981); "The Role of Lament in the Theology of the Old Testament," *Interpretation* 28(1974) 32-38. Walter Brueggemann has written several articles: "From Hurt to Joy, From Death to Life," *Interpretation* 28 (1974) 3-19; "Formfulness of Grief," *Interpretation* 31(1977) 263-75; "Psalms and the Life of Faith: A Suggested Typology of Function," *Journal for the Study of the Old Testament* 17(1980) 3-32.

18. Interestingly, Westermann had originally titled the work that became *Praise and Lament in the Psalms* as only *The Praise of God in the Psalms* (Atlanta: John Knox, 1965).

19. See bibliography in note 17, and "Reservoirs of Unreason," *Reformed Liturgy and Music* 17(1983) 91-104.

20. For bibliography and discussion of the issues, see Sigmund Mowinckel, *The Psalms in Israel's Worship* (Nashville: Abingdon Press, 1962) vol. II, 53-73, and W. H. Bellinger, Jr., *Psalmody and Prophecy* (JSOT Supplement Series 27; Sheffield, U.K.: JSOT Press, 1984) 78-82.

21. John Goldingay, "The Dynamic Cycle of Praise and Prayer in the Psalms," *Journal for the Study of the Old Testament* 20(1981) 85-90.

22. Brevard Childs, *Introduction to the Old Testament as Scripture* (Philadelphia: Fortress, 1979) 504-25.

23. John F. Craghan, *The Psalms: Prayers for the Ups, Downs and In-betweens of Life* (Wilmington, Michael Glazier, Inc., 1985) 166-67.

24. See the article by Sparkes and Rutherford, note 16; also Reginald Fuller, "Lectionary for Funerals," *Worship* 56(1982) 36-63; Robert Hoeffner, "A Pastoral Evaluation of the Rite of Funerals," *Worship* 55(1981) 482-99.

25. See the *Order of Christian Funerals*.

26. See Robert Krieg, "The Funeral Homily: A Theological View," *Worship* 58(1984) 222-39.

Death Rituals and Life Values: The American Way

MARY DOMBECK

The death of President Kennedy on November 22, 1963, was like an earthquake. It set off tremors of emotion across the country, and the ritual activity generated held the whole country entranced participating in the shock and the loss through the news media.

It was at that time, when I was a young foreign exchange student, and, although I didn't know it at the time, a budding anthropologist, that I became forced to look at myself, and at the place I had just left, with an objectivity I had not known before. We take things for granted about our own society, and we accept cultural rationalizations as the only valid explanations for what is going on. Cross-cultural experience shows us the peculiarity of our own point of view, and enables us to see our own customs and those of other societies in a new perspective.

So I participated with others, mourning the snuffing out of the life of this vibrant man, who, I was told, was the youngest of all Presidents and the first Catholic President of the United States, by following the events in the news media with my friends and neighbors. I followed the body from the hospital in Dallas, to Air Force I where his successor was sworn in to the office of the Presidency, to the cathedral and to the capitol rotunda in Washington and the processions to the grave site at Arlington National Cemetery. It was the widow who intrigued me. This young, beautiful, fashionable lady, with not a crease in her clothing, not a hair out of place, who always looked tragically sad yet stoically composed. While I did not expect her to tear off her clothes as widows did in other societies that I knew, I wondered whether she cried herself to sleep, and why her eyes were not swollen with tears. Was her emotional control related to the fact that she had been the wife of the chief executive or just to the fact that she was an American? I asked my American friends and neighbors, but they could only answer that she was exemplary. It was, they said, her fortitude and strength that was holding her family, her country, and even themselves together. The fact that she kept herself from "breaking down" was evidence of her superior courage and leadership. They needed her self-control as much as they needed to know that there had been orderly transfer of power and responsibility. These qualities which they saw in her captured qualities most highly valued at a time of great danger.

At this time, I would like to read a passage from the experience of another widow, this one Baba of Karo, a woman of the Muslim Hausa, daughter of a Koranic teacher, married to a Koranic scholar (Smith, 1954, 1981):

> Two days later he died . . . We were there together, I, and my co-wife and our children; she had been pregnant for a long time and ten days later she bore Audi. We wailed, we threw ourselves down on the ground, we wailed and wept. The next morning we sent a boy to tell Hasana, when she came she wailed and wailed that her brother was dead. Everyone in

the town collected and all the *malams* (Koranic scholars). After three days his kinsfolk and our kinsfolk and the town people came to greet us, after seven days they distributed alms to the *malams*. The *malams* came too, to recite the prayers; they were given our husband's clothes, and food and money. On the fortieth day the alms are finished. We remained in mourning for a hundred and thirty days.

When you are in mourning you boil water every Friday morning, you make it very hot, and you go behind your huts and wash your body. Every day you do your ordinary ablutions before you say your prayers. When your husband dies, you must wail if you loved him, then you are sad at heart also, he isn't there . . . If you didn't particularly like him, you wail because of compassion, you had got used to him and now he isn't here. Ah Allah preserve us in health! (Smith, 1954, 1981, pp. 211-212).

When comparing the expression of emotion at funerals in different societies, we assume that relationships in all societies produce feelings of attachment, and that the termination of these attachments produce emotional distress. But the way those emotions are expressed verbally and nonverbally is unique to each social group.

Several questions arise when considering a society as large, complex, and composed of so many different ethnic groups as the United States:

1) Do we find uniformity in funerary customs and death rituals in a society which historically and actually contains such ethnic diversity?

2) If there is uniformity in the midst of diversity what might funerary customs and death rituals tell us about life values in this society?

3) Finally, how do the customs and rituals transform the fact of physical death into social, religious, and spiritual reality for the participants?

UNIFORMITY IN THE MIDST OF DIVERSITY

The two examples given above illustrate two important points which can be used as a springboard for the discussion of uniformity in the midst of diversity. First, death is a universal experience of humankind because of its basic part in human biology and psychology. Death has an impact on people in all societies. We can assume that all societies mark the fact of death by special events, that all societies have ways to dispose of dead bodies, and that all societies have ways to continue with life. But beyond those universals there is immense variability:

> Corpses are burned or buried, with, or without animal or human sacrifice; they are preserved by smoking, embalming, freezing or pickling. They are eaten ritually, exposed as carrion, abandoned or dismembered. Funerals are the occasion for avoiding people or for holding rowdy parties, for abstaining from sex, or for having sexual orgies, and for showing the whole gamut of emotions (Huntington and Metcalf, 1979, p. 1).

My point is that ethnic diversity in the United States should be considered in the context of human universality and cross-cultural variability. Jackie and Baba both demonstrated emotions, but the style and intensity of the expression of those emotions is socially constructed and sanctioned.

Second, death rituals express social values and also educate participants and members of that society about those values. Not only did the presidential funeral provide an instructive illustration of American values as expressed through the ritual, but also Americans learned about death, about funerals, and about their values by observing and participating in the funeral. Death rituals are models *of* and models *for* a society (Geertz, 1973, pp. 87-125). Therefore the funerals of kings and chief executives which many observe and in which many participated are paradigmatic of the regular aspects of funerals in a society (Huntington and Metcalf, 1979, pp. 121-52).

Functions of Death Rituals

When I ask Americans why they think funerals are necessary, the most frequent answers I receive are related to the following functions:

a) Managing the emotions which arise.
    "Because we were so sad."
    "Because people feel guilty."
b) Managing dependence on others.
    "I wouldn't have known what to do without their help at a time like this."
    "It brought many people together to help my mother."
c) Announcing finality and emphasizing the meaningfulness of life.
    "You have to make a production of it; you can't just throw people in the ground."
    "We wanted the world to know that our baby had lived even though for only a few days."
d) Announcing the changes in role structure.
    "It helped us to go on with our lives without him. We had to take on his work."

It would be helpful to look at the functions of death rituals in the context of human universality and cross cultural variability, in order to discover whether there is uniformity in death customs and rituals in the United States. My resources are surveys and ethnographic studies done in the United States and in other societies.

(a) Emotions

In a study by Rosenblatt, Walsh, and Jackson (1976), seventy-eight societies were measured for emotionality variables. In seventy-seven of these, the United States among them, some kind of emotion was judged to be present by independent raters, for bereaved persons in the society. In the seventy-seven societies studied, anger and sadness were identified. There were gender differences in the expression of emotion. In most of the societies women expressed more sadness, and men expressed more anger and aggression. One of the hypotheses of that study with regard to the expression of anger and aggression is that the earlier, and more important the involvement of ritual specialists, the less the expression of anger and aggression during mourning. In the United States there is a high level of control of emotions, especially of anger and aggression, during death rites. According to this hypothesis, this is related to the early involvement of physicians, clergy, and funeral directors. In fact, the general involvement of funeral establishments and funeral directors in a high percentage (90-92 percent) of deaths and death rituals (Dempsey, 1975) is one of the points of uniformity in the United States (Rosenblatt et al., 1976).

We think of Baba of Karo who tells us that she is supposed to wail out of compassion for her dead husband and of Jackie Kennedy whose silent and controlled sadness was an inspiration to Americans at a time of danger. It is clear that Americans value control and are not given to the expression of intense "irrational" or of negative emotion even at a time when they feel it.

(b) *Dependence*

Managing dependence on others is a practical problem at the time of death. The system of dependencies are interrupted and sometimes overturned. The sudden death of a person on whom others depended makes it difficult for the daily routine to be maintained. Chronic and catastrophic illness, however, brings with it other dependencies, such as to health officials. In the United States the announcer and pronouncer of death is the physician, the setting of death is often the hospital (Sudnow, 1967). Also, as mentioned earlier there is almost certain involvement of funeral establishments. There are no secular death rituals analogous to being married by the justice of the peace. Even unchurched Americans want a ceremony at death. Funeral establishments usually have chapels for such purposes. It is important to note that at a time when emotions are so intense and control is so valued, there is very great need for death rituals and a great openness to involvement with the church and church representatives. Death can initiate or revive involvement with church.

There have been many studies and writing about the role of funeral directors in American society since the famous exposé by Jessica Mitford in *The American Way of Death* (1963). The ambivalence toward funeral directors and their industry continues; however, the wide use of their services also continues. They seem to provide information, skills and comfort which Americans want. In fact, most Americans take the practice of embalming for granted, believing it to be legally required although it is not.

> Given the myriad variety of death rites throughout the world, and the cultural heterogeneity of American society, the expectation is that funeral practices will vary widely from one region or social class to another . . . The odd fact is that they do not. The overall form of funerals is remarkably uniform from coast to coast. Its general features include: rapid removal of the corpse to a funeral parlor, embalming, institutionalized "viewing" and disposal by burial (Huntington and Metcalf, 1979, p. 187).

In a society where autonomy, individualism and independence are highly valued, dependence is tolerated and accepted by most Americans at the time of death. Not only dependence on family and friends, but especially dependence on specialists who "know what to do at a time like this."

(c) *Finality and Meaningfulness*

Death is an event which challenges individual understanding and expresses social ideologies. Persons, as well as societies, spend much effort in explaining the phenomenon. Even the alleged "denial of death" in America could be a way of dealing with death so that finality and meaningfulness are expressed (Dempsey, 1972, pp. 33-64). Americans are concerned with the making of wills, the buying of insurance, the buying of burial insurance and of cemetery plots. All of these activities are ways of anticipating death. They all have a future time orientation. Death rituals also are ways in which societies attempt to explain the finality of life as well as its meaningfulness.

Bronislaw Malinowski (1948, 1959) describes ceremonials of death as religious acts distinguishable from magical and functional (technical) acts. His analysis of what he saw among the natives of the Trobriand Islands is brilliant and eloquent:

> The ceremonials of death which ties the survivors to the body and rivets them to the place of death, the beliefs in the existence of the spirit, in its beneficent influences or malevolent intention, in the duties of a series of commemorative or sacrificial ceremonies—in all this religion counteracts the centrifugal forces of fear, dismay, demoralization and provides the most powerful means of reintegration of the group's shaken solidarity and the reestablishment of its morale (Malinowski, 1948, 1958, p. 52).

Death rituals like other religious rituals are born out of the disparity between human aspiration and human reality. According to Malinowski, rituals relieve anxiety and give comfort to individuals and draw communities together at a time when tragedy threatened to disintegrate them. Rituals are prescribed symbolic acts which are repetitive and satisfy a sense of appropriateness. Rituals can relabel a situation, allow for the expression of feelings, proclaim the present social order, or effect a transformation. Social relations can be expressed and confirmed when rituals are enacted.

Funerals are life-crisis rituals (Turner, 1967, pp. 7-9). A life-crisis ritual is an important point in the physical or social development of an individual, such as birth, puberty, marriage, or death. In most societies there are ceremonies to mark the transition from one phase of life or social status to another. At times of personal and social disorganization, a ritual provides the need for order and allows for the expression of feeling and, as Malinowski observes, relieves anxiety.

Another explanation of the function of rituals appears to complement Malinowski's; Radcliffe-Brown suggests that the social function of funeral rites is to *create* a feeling of solemnity and anxiety (Radcliffe-Brown 1965, pp. 148-49) in order to emphasize the reality of insecurity and danger, to reaffirm social stability, and to give a social explanation of death. When my young informant said to me, "You have to have a funeral when someone dies: you have to make a production of it, you can't just throw people in the ground," he may have been thinking about it in that way.

In a land where busyness and productive activity is valued, in a society where the future is the preferred time orientation, my informant recognizes that it is important to pause and contemplate a death with anxiety and sadness, to proclaim in the present that a life has existed in the past, and that that life is meaningful.

Rituals mark time. In some agricultural societies the festival of the dead also serves to mark out the agricultural cycle (Bloch and Parry, 1982, pp. 9-15). Rituals act as boundary markers creating intervals in social life which break up linear duration. Our lives are not marked emotionally by the calendar and the clock but by the little rituals of waking, washing, eating, and going to sleep at night. The rituals of death intensify what we already know very well: that in the midst of our daily life we encounter death (the end of life as we know it). We also learn that living continues—an occasion is created in which duration is transformed into a timeless memorial: "When my dad died," "when the baby was buried," "when I finished school," "the Christmas of 1963! that was the Christmas after Kennedy died." These are all events marked by ritual. A funeral can mark the end of an era and the beginning of another for a person, for a family, for a community, or for a nation. "We talk of measuring time as if it were a concrete thing waiting to be measured, but, in fact, we create time by creating intervals in social life" (Leach 1961, p. 135).

All funerals remind us of other funerals and also make us think of our own death. Thus while finality is announced, meaningfulness is proclaimed. Death rituals affirm that life is precious and significant in the face of human vulnerability and insignificance.

In many societies symbols of rebirth and fertility are integral parts of funeral rituals (Bloch and Parry, 1982). Death is associated with the renewal of life demonstrated in the renewal of people, of animals and of crops. In those societies, mostly agricultural, there is not a very high ideological value placed on individuality. As people die, so new people are born; as vegetation dies, so it is reborn. Like the seasons, as death is expected to follow birth, so birth is expected to follow death. Time is cyclical and repetitive, and in this way a sense of timelessness is achieved.

A Western person has trouble with this kind of transcendence of death. In the West a person is born at a precise time on a calendar date, and that same person is expected to die at a precise time on a calendar date. The name and the exact date is marked on the tombstone. The exact times and dates are recorded on birth and death certificates. At the time of death it is not satisfactory that another person will be born soon. Westerners value individuality and have a sense of history. This is a historical understanding of time, not a cyclical one.

Christianity begins with historical events, always retains a historical perspective and attempts to transcend linear duration not by a cyclical repetitive sense of time but by the memorial time.

Death is at the very center of the Christian faith. The central event is the death and resurrection of a historical person. Therefore, when John Doe loses his wife, a unique individual who lived from 1920–1987, he knows that he does not understand rationally what happened to her, that he will not understand until maybe when he himself dies. The Christian death rite tells him to look at the fact of this loss in the context of one particular individual who lived for thirty-three years, approximately 1954 years ago, died, was buried, and was resurrected. These facts are not explained, they are just remembered and celebrated. In fact they are not only celebrated at death but also throughout the year at every sad and glad occasion. Because death and life are remembered every day, it is possible that life can also be remembered at the time of death. The Christian story was created by memorials of a life, a death, and a resurrection; life is made meaningful by remembering the story, therefore the participant can expect that life can continue to be created by the memorial at this death of Jane Doe.

The central rituals of the Christian faith are the rituals at the Easter season. These rituals celebrate the following events in Christ's life. His decision to die, his anguish in the face of his mortality, the ugly spectacle of his death, the burial, the time of vigil when he was in the tomb, the resurrection, a time of appearances when he was on earth but not in the same way, and a time when he reaches his final destination, while his spirit takes the community by storm. There is not only one rite, but there are a series of rites that last many weeks, and all of this is remembered regularly by memorial celebrations.[1]

It is a notable fact that although the Easter story contains several distinct rituals lasting days, weeks, and months, the Christian funeral has different steps, yet they are not separated into discrete rituals spanning a long period of time.

When this fact is explored and examined in the context of cross-cultural variability, it becomes another point of uniformity in death customs and rituals in the United States, namely, that in this nation it is not a general custom to have multiple or even dual death rituals.

Many societies (75 percent of the societies studied by Rosenblatt and his associates) have multiple funeral ceremonies. Notably there are final ceremonies which occur days, weeks, months, or even, though rarely, years after the death.

A final ceremony is a public formal ritual where the deceased receives special remembrance and attention. These are not simply occasions when all the dead are remembered at the same annual ritual, but special rituals where a particular person is remembered. In some societies this is also the occasion of a second burial, and in many societies, the final ceremonies herald the end of mourning (Rosenblatt et al., 1976, pp. 923-93).

> After a hundred and thirty days a widow comes out of mourning. That night she does not sleep, there is drumming on calabashes until the morning. The morning comes and she bathes herself, she dresses in a new blouse, a new cloth, a new head-kerchief. She takes off her old clothes and gives them as alms to an old woman. Everyone in your kin and in your husband's kin comes with alms—guinea corn, rice, millet, money. You prepare porridge and *cuge,* the *malams* come and recite the prayers, and you distribute food to them and send it round the compounds. At Azahar everyone who has come for the prayers and greetings gets up and goes home. If the woman is young, not an old lady like me, that same day that the *malams* have recited the last prayers they also recite the marriage verses and she is married again (Smith, 1954, p. 217).

Thus for Baba as well as for widows in other societies, with multiple death ceremonies, the designated time for bereavement is interwoven in the death ceremonies; the rituals are extended over a longer period of time, and have a formal ending in the final ceremony. Mourning is intensified and yet time-limited (Rosenblatt et al., 1976, p. 94).

In the United States where individuality is valued and time is marked historically in terms of linear calendar time with a preference for a future orientation, a particular person's life is viewed as extending in a straight line which begins at birth and ends with death. Then there is one brief ceremony. For Americans the time allowed for mourning is shortened and, at the same time, not limited.

When John Doe loses his wife, at the completion of the funeral, after the weekend, when all his family go back to their homes, he is exhorted to go back to his usual activities. When the time of memories come like dinner time, her birthday, his birthday, Christmas, their anniversary, there may or may not be a family member, friend, or even a member of the church community with him. But there is no formal public ceremony, or the expectation of a future ceremony, where he can publicly take his place again as bereaved, dependent, and at the place of mystery. His close relatives who knew Jane may talk about her, but others will be embarrassed by his grief and reluctant to talk about something which is not given social permission. The end of the mourning period is not defined and when it does come, ritually speaking he is alone.

It is not surprising that in societies which do not have dual or final ceremonies, grief is prolonged:

> The presence of final ceremonies was strongly associated with the global measure of grief after the end of mourning. Where final ceremonies were present, prolonged grief was less likely to be present or frequent; where final ceremonies were absent, prolonged grief was more likely to be present or frequent. Thus, as hypothesized, final ceremonies seem to serve the function of time-limiting grief (Rosenblatt, et al., 1976, p. 93).

CHANGES IN THE SOCIAL ORDER

When my informant tells me that the funeral "helps to go on with our lives without him," he may be talking about the importance of being allowed to express grief, or he may be talking about the funeral helping to strengthen the commitment to the fact that the dead man is now gone and that social reality is changed. A death effects a change in personal reality and also in social reality. It is a time of transformation.

The ritual is supposed to effect and proclaim that he who was a living man is now a dead man, that the wife is transformed into a widow, the child into an orphan. Wills can be read; property can change hands. Old commitments are discharged; new commitments are acquired; alliances and enmities are rearranged.

The funerals of chief executives illustrate this well. In the airplane that carried the body of one President, the new President took the oath of office. There must be a President by the time Washington is reached. In the medieval political system, the saying was, "The king is dead, long live the king!" There had to be a connection between the "Body natural" as mortal man, and his "Body politic" as an immortal office (Kantorowicz, E. 1957), and yet the man who dies is not totally identified with his office. The man is dead but the office remains. The word "office" is used in social theory to indicate a role or status. But it comes from the theological idea of "call," work, profession, vocation (Fortes, 1962).

The office of king or President is paradigmatic of other roles and statuses. For example, the role and status of widow, orphan, widower, older son, only living relative, mother of a dead child are formidable responsibilities which demand commitment. Through ritual, office can be "entrusted to the holder in a binding manner, or again, conversely legitimately stripped from him" (Fortes, 1962, p. 86).

The funeral is a rite-of-passage. According to Van Gennep (1901, 1960) a rite-of-passage is a ritual which facilitates and transforms the participant from one state to another. The ritual has three parts, starting with separation from one status and ending with reincorporation into a new status. In between those two there is a time of marginality, when one passes through the "limen" or threshold (Turner, 1967). At the time of liminality one is symbolically "neither here nor there" in the social order. Moreover, the social order seems to be turned upside down. The privileged have lost their privileges, and new privileges are expected, but are not yet a reality. It is at the funeral where people talk of role changes. The mother is dead. Who will take care of the children? The father will have to be father and mother. Maybe the grandmother and aunt will help.

In some societies this dual process of separation and reincorporation is mirrored in beliefs about the fate of the soul and the ritual condition of the mourners. It finds expression in the idea of a dangerous period when the departed is socially uncontrollable or potentially malevolent (Bloch and Parry, 1983, p. 4). The funeral is seen as a rite of passage, a journey for the living, and also for the dead. If the dead have not quite completed the crossing, then they might be able, though dead, to interfere in the land of the living. This gives rise to a great fear of ghosts. The fear and the cognition of ghosts is a cross-cultural and universal experience. Yet there is pressure on Americans who are bereaved, because of the American value on rationality and logic, to question their own sanity if they experience such things. They will keep these experiences to themselves, thus increasing their isolation. Or if they find an understanding friend, relative, pastor, or therapist, they will say: "I hope you don't think I'm crazy but I saw him. He was standing at the foot of my bed and he was smiling. I was comforted," or "I was scared!"

Yet the Christian story is replete with journey motifs, liminality statements, and understandings of the establishment of a new order. In fact, the gospel itself, the life, death, resurrection, and coming again of the Christ is such a story. There is a journey to Jerusalem which is the beginning of a journey which will unite the Father and the Son; there are the statements of reversal. Christ is the "first fruits of those who died." The earthly order is compared to the spiritual order. The present kingdom is compared to the Kingdom of God where the last are first, and where one is expected to be reborn like a child. When Jesus appears after death, his disciples have to be reassured that he is not a ghost. The whole Easter cycle from Passion Sunday to Pentecost would be, and sometimes in actuality is, a wonderfully comforting series of rituals for the bereaved. It would be a way where the memorial of the life of Christ can be the context and setting of grieving all losses and celebrating all gains. Yet the average American, Catholic or otherwise, has one short funeral in the presence of community. For Americans grieving is private. Unreasonable experiences are kept to oneself; anniversaries and other memorials are, if not totally private, certainly not public. The bereaved who were allowed circumspect dependence on ritual specialists are now expected to continue to function as usual without "breaking down."

Actually some communities do continue to surround the bereaved with comfort, using rituals like the Eucharist, memorial services, and healing services for this purpose. But there is no public expectation that there will be such rituals long after the funeral. If there are, the notices are not as public as the obituaries and the notices of the funeral.

Even if one were to look at the stages of the American Christian funeral as a rite-of-passage, it would not be a complete one. There is certainly a journey from the hospital to the funeral home, a journey to the church, and finally a journey to the gravesite. This happens in a short time. Moreover, seldom do the bereaved get to observe and participate in the actual lowering of the body into the grave. I have asked several bereaved persons why they think this is so. The most common answer I receive is: "If they would actually put the body underground, many people there would 'lose it.' " In fact, those who do "lose it" anyway at the gravesite are exhorted by others to control themselves.[2]

There is one more aspect of the American funeral that I would like to address, and that is the treatment of the dead body. We have already established that cross-cultural variability in the way dead bodies are treated is immense and that for the United States in over 90 percent of the cases the overall form of funerals involves the rapid removal of the body to a funeral parlor, embalming, "viewing," and disposal by burial. There are certainly variations from these norms. There are variations on whether the body will be "viewed" or not and for how many days before burial. Cremation is now an option,[3] in few instances, and some families are exercising the option of bringing the body home for the wake. Yet these are all variations on the same themes. Embalming is considered the norm, and by many it is believed to be legally required.

It might have been helpful, if time permitted, to have followed the history of embalming in the United States in order to place these comments in context. This can only be done in a very cursory fashion at this time.

As hospitals became the usual place where people died, as churches no longer had cemeteries on their grounds, as the mobility of Americans increased, it became customary to improve the looks of the body, especially for the sake of the relative who came from far. During the Civil War, it became the custom to ship corpses long distances to their homes (that was indeed what happened to President Lincoln's body). The explanation given for embalming is that it is important to remember one's loved one at their best, not in the horrible state of putrescence and decay. When Americans allow their loved ones to be embalmed, it is not to preserve the body indefinitely in a mummified state, as the ancient Egyptians used to do, it is, rather, just to postpone decay until after the short funeral. Sociologists and anthropologists have not agreed on the same analyses about why embalming is wanted. The explanation is given about Americans' preoccupation with health and hygiene. This explanation is certainly notable. It agrees with the general aversion that Americans have with all body odors. But what about the way the body is dressed? the expression sought on the face of the deceased? and the setting, the flowers, the inside of the coffin?

A man who saw Lincoln in the coffin reported:

I saw him in his coffin. The face was the same as in life. Death had not changed the kindly countenance in any line. There was upon it the same sad look that it had worn always, though not so intensely sad as it had been in life. It was as if the spirit had come to the poor clay, reshaped the wonderful sweet face, and given it an expression of gladness . . . It was the look of a worn man suddenly relieved (Quoted in Huntington and Metcalf, 1979, 206 from Hamilton and Ostendorf, 1963, p. 2340).

What this man sought in the dead President's face was relief from suffering. In fact, when viewing the body, it is customary to make a comment on how good the body looks, how peaceful it looks, and, if appropriate, something about being glad for the end of the suffering. "He is at rest." The indication is that the rest is a well-deserved goal, a balancing goal after strife and suffering. In a society where autonomy and self-determination are valued and aggression and violence is a reality in life, peace and rest are sought at death. This was certainly true of American society from colonial days, frontier days, the Civil War, and the other wars that have been fought since. It is true that in medieval and post-medieval Catholicism the prayer was for salvation from the sufferings of hell and purgatory. "Eternal rest grant unto them, O Lord"; "Deliver me, O Lord, from eternal death and from that terrible day." However, when someone says, "He looks peaceful, his sufferings are ended," he or she does not mean the sufferings of hell, but the sufferings of earth.

To summarize, the themes which have emerged are as follows:

At the time of death, control is valued and needed. Americans are not given to the expression of intense negative emotions, even when these emotions are felt. There is a high value placed on rationality and logic, and "unreasonable" feelings and thoughts are difficult to express.

Dependence is tolerated and accepted, especially dependence on experts and ritual specialists, but only for a short time.

There is only one funeral, though there are many parts to it. It is the exception when the funeral spans a week. It is usually shorter, namely, about three to four days. After that, the bereaved are expected to return to their regular activity. There is no special social marking of death beyond that, and the private experience of grief is not limited by time.

The body is prepared to postpone decay until after the funeral, and there is a general preference for viewing the body in a quiet surrounding. The deceased is expected to look comfortable, clean, calm, and rested. Experiences of the deceased by the bereaved after death are played down.

LIFE VALUES IN AMERICAN SOCIETIES

Funerary customs and death rituals highlight the following values:

Emotional control is valued in the face of emotional stress.

Reasonableness, rationality, and logic are valued in the face of experiences which defy logic like the experience of encountering the deceased after death.

Autonomy and individuality are valued; dependence on others is measured and allowed only for a short time.

Individuality and privacy are valued. The experience of grief is a private one for the most part.

Time is measured historically and linearly, and the preferred time orientation is the future. The future is valued, but at the same time there is difficulty in the philosophical problem created by regarding death as the end of the line. Although the Christian story is historical, proclaims memorials in time, and does not regard death as the end, Americans seem to have difficulty reconciling these two ideologies.

Americans value rituals, even rituals which are secular. However, at the time of death there is openness to involvement with church or with religion. Religious death rituals are wanted.

Americans value balance. Where there is suffering and violence in life there is a compensatory need for calm, peacefulness, and rest at death.

ETHNICITY

I have not explored any particular ethnic group yet. This has not been because there are no differences in those groups. It is, however, true that the uniformity of American death rituals is remarkable in the face of such diversity and in a country so large. Moreover, the United States has continued to receive immigrants from different societies who have brought their own customs from the old country. However, most of them after two generations begin to adopt American practices like embalming and the engaging of funeral specialists at the time of death. Or, they feel the pressure to do so. The differences noted in the ethnic groups are variations on the uniform themes that have occurred in our reflections of death rituals and life values in America.

A priest friend of mine who is second generation Italian has told me that when he has to go to an Irish wake, whenever possible he goes with an Irish priest brother. It helps him to go with someone who can handle what he perceives to be superficial levity but is learning to understand as a legitimate expression of grief. At the same time his friend asks him to come to Italian funerals and family gatherings, because he cannot handle what he perceives as unbearable dramatics. It is helpful to be with someone who understands the emotional language. There are indeed communities where the language is different, for example, the recently immigrated Italian communities in New York cities, Irish communities in Boston, Mexican communities in Southern

California and Texas, rural communities in West Virginia, Puerto Rican communities in New York City, Polish communities in Chicago, and Black communities in New Orleans and other large cities.

If the minister, lay or ordained, understands the ethnic background, it is very comforting, not only that someone understands and remembers the customs, but also, the pressure to change them, which comes from within the ethnic community itself. If, however, the minister finds himself or herself in a community alien to his or her own background, then there is an opportunity to become more sensitive. Each one of these communities deserves the perceptive scrutiny of a person who is having a cross-cultural experience. The cross-cultural experience makes the analytic anthropologist or the perceptive traveler ask: "What makes them do or say a peculiar thing like that?" This is immediately followed by: "What we do must seem peculiar to them; where are the universals? How can I put my own values in perspective?" It is this kind of cross-cultural dialogue which transcends ethnocentrism. When one is ethnocentric, one adopts a simplistic tour-book approach to people in different societies. A simplistic approach attempts to interact with another society without changing one's own perspective or one's own values. Ethnocentrism is defined as "a habitual disposition to judge foreign peoples or groups by the standards and practices of one's own culture or ethnic group." Another description of ethnocentrism comes in the form of an excellent proverb: "An ass who travels returns an ass!" Presumably, the cross-cultural experience is intended to make one human, like Apulius' golden ass who was transformed into a human being after the mystery rites (Apulius translated by R. Graves, 1951).

Ethnocentrism often results in thinking that one's own customs and beliefs are better than others. However, a very subtle form of ethnocentrism results in thinking that practices of others are better than one's own. For example, in comparing Baba of Karo and Jacqueline Kennedy, one might be tempted to say: "It is more natural to cry and wail than to be stoical when a loved one dies; natural is better, so we will all be better off if we let our feelings out."

This kind of comparison might result in adding to a bereaved person's pressures by the subtle message that they ought to be acting in a way that is alien to their own. In fact, these are the kinds of messages that many immigrants receive within their own ethnic groups in their struggle to fit into American society. Usually by the third generation after immigration the American customs are adopted (Zborowski, 1969). Only communities who have a continuing flow of incoming immigrants retain many ethnic customs. In ethnic communities the pressures are augmented by the struggle between the generations. A death typically brings out the struggle between the desire for the ways of the land of the future and the poignant nostalgia for the ways of the land of the past.

It is important for the minister to remember that much of the pressure comes from inside the community itself. A sensitive ear and a few well-placed questions are more helpful than a problem-solving approach.

Let me give an example: (This is a true story. Some of the details and the names are changed.)

Miss Strain is a second generation American who has just lost her mother after a long, difficult, and debilitating illness. Her mother spent the last two years of her life in a nursing home. Her father has been dead for many years, and her relationship with her mother was very important. She has no siblings and she never married. Her mother has left her no instructions about the funeral, and was so mentally and physically deteriorated that no such instructions were possible. Miss Strain's circle of friends have convinced her that cremation of the body is what she ought to do. They tell her it is less difficult than to have to stare at an image of her mother looking like a "painted doll" in the casket. Miss Strain is caught between the opinions of her friends who have been very supportive during the time of her mother's illness and the opinions of her Aunt Faith and her Uncle Loyal who are first generation Americans and who still belong to the old ethnic parish where her mother grew up. Uncle Loyal is her mother's brother and is ill himself. Aunt Faith, who has always been nice to her, is upset because she says cremation is wrong: "It is surprising that the Church would allow it to happen, and, wouldn't old Grandma Prudence turn in her grave?" Miss Strain is exhausted by her mother's long illness and numbed by the reality of her mother's death. She wants to do the right thing. There will be many people at the funeral, including her Aunt Critical on her father's side.

Miss Strain is not a regular church-goer, but she is a member in good standing. Father Upright has told her kindly but firmly that the ashes cannot be brought into the church during the funeral service. There is also the Compassionate Committee from church who occasionally came to visit her mother in the nursing home. Sister Solace is part of the Compassionate Committee. Somebody on the committee was concerned because it is more difficult to grieve when you don't see the body. Miss Strain has seen her mother's dead body in the nursing home but no one else has. She wants to do the right thing not only for herself but for her relatives. However, she remembers what her friends and peers have told her about the body in the casket looking like a "painted doll." She misses her mother, not the way her mother had become after the long illness, but the way she used to be before she became ill. She is also caught between two generations, two sets of customs, and the psychologically sound opinions of the educated people on the Compassionate Committee, the exhaustion of the illness and the paralysis of her grief. She hardly has any feelings beyond exhaustion.

It is at this time that a sensitive ear, and a few sensitive questions are more helpful than a problem-solving approach. Questions or statements like: "When was the last funeral you attended?" "What happened?" "What kind of an experience was it?" "Tell me about your father's funeral." "Have you been to a funeral when someone was cremated?"

Whichever way Miss Strain decides, she needs a ritual which will speak to her grief, reach the core of her life questions, and help her in the transformation of herself in light of her mother's death. Actually she chose cremation. The decision was the only one she could make at the time because of the many pressures from all sides and because of her emotional paralysis. What she needs most of all is for lines of communications to be kept open between herself and her church community so that, after the funeral, when the grieving period is just beginning she can talk about and reflect on what happened at the funeral. She needs the opportunity to articulate her thoughts on the death, the funeral, and her faith, and maybe even voice her desire for other memorials.

This example illustrates the tensions and pressures present in an ethnic group. Each group is different. There is no way to predict a particular set of customs, to anticipate specific issues or have protocol solutions. That is because much depends on the particular setting, the year of ethnicity, the influence of new immigrants, and the particular group's relationship to the Church. There are in each group conflicting pressures to resist American social values and much stronger pressures to conform to them.

At this point it would be useful to comment on two particular ethnic groups, namely, Black Americans and Hispanics. The reason to focus on Black Americans is that they present a paradigmatic view of customs valued by all Americans.

My sources are some interviews in Rochester and a study by Kalisch and Reynolds (1976). The Kalisch and Reynolds study was conducted by doing community surveys, newspaper analysis, interviews of professionals, such as nurses, physicians, funeral directors, and participant observation.

Funerals are extremely important for Black Americans. A significantly larger number of Black Americans had taken out life insurance than other ethnic groups in the study. Some of the coverage insured funeral costs, embalming, and burial. There is a very high value placed on having a "good funeral" which is "done right." The corpse must look dignified and especially serene and peaceful. Black Americans prefer not to use euphemisms for talking about death. Black writings and Black music portray death in stark immediacy. More Black Americans in the sample had had a recent encounter with death than subjects of any other ethnic group in the study.

Black Americans adopt the Anglo ideology with regard to dependency on experts and respond to questions about the value of controlling one's feelings by valuing self-control as do Anglo Americans. However, observers at funerals state that Black Americans have an expressive style which allows them to express intense feelings despite efforts to exert self-restraint.

Hispanics represent 40 percent of Catholics in the United States. Hispanics do not comprise one group. They are from Panama, Guatemala, Cuba, Mexico, and Puerto Rico. As with all ethnic groups the particular setting, generation of ethnicity, the influence of new immigrants, the relationship with the new country and the Church are important considerations.

However, it is important to note that a higher percentage of Hispanics have been in the United States for less time and do not speak English than other ethnic groups in the study (Kalish and Reynolds, 1976). Moreover, among American Hispanics more young people could speak the old language than young people of other ethnic groups. Moreover, there is more intra-group consistency relative to age, gender, and education regarding opinions about death rituals and customs than other ethnic groups in the study.

Hispanic Americans feel free to express their feelings at funerals. They tend to depend more on family and community than specialists. The influence of the Church is very important in life as well as in death because Hispanics are family-centered and Church-centered.[4]

In summary, while Black American communities present a paradigmatic view of death custom valued by all Americans, Hispanic Americans represent those communities most reluctant and slow to change their own customs in favor of Anglo customs. These remarks are suggested by the Kalish and Reynolds study (1976) and are presented here as a hypothesis which needs to be investigated further.

HOW RITUALS TRANSFORM

For my analysis of death rituals, I refer to the work of Victor Turner who did his ethnographic work among the Ndembu of Zambia. While observing life crisis rituals celebrated by the people, he became aware of the importance of key symbols which he identified as *dominant ritual symbols.*

Ritual symbols are the smallest and ultimate units of a ritual. Ritual symbols are pieces of ritual. Since a symbol typifies, and represents something by possession of analogous qualities, symbols are usually empirically observable. They are: objects, activities, events, gestures, relationships, and spatial units.

Symbols have the property of condensing many meanings into one referent. Not only are there many referents or signifiers but also the symbol has the power to unite all of those even though they appear to be polarized. At the one pole the symbol has sensory properties; at the other end of the pole it is ideological. For example, the symbol of the *mudhi tree* is such a symbol for the Ndembu of Zambia. At the sensory pole it refers simply to the milk-tree (because of its white sap). *Mudhi* also refers to milk, the breasts of the young initiate. It is called the "tree of mother and child." Women are initiated under the *mudhi-tree,* and men are circumcised under it. However, a Ndembu will also say that a "tribesman drinks from the breast of the tribal customs." Because the tribe is matrilineal, the tribal chief is referred to as *Mudhi*—the mother of the people. This meaning represents the ideological pole of the symbol. At the sensory pole the symbol evokes physical desire or physical horror, and at the opposite pole the symbol is normative; it evokes social and religious value. It tends to stress the harmonious and cohesive aspects of social relationships and to integrate social action.

> The disparate significata are inter-connected by virtue of their possession of their common possession of analogous qualities or by association in fact or thought. Such qualities or links of association may in themselves be quite trivial or random or widely distributed among a range of phenomena. Their very generality enables them to bracket together the most diverse ideas and phenomena. Thus, as we have seen the milk tree stands for, *inter alia*, women's breasts, motherhood, a novice at NKang'a, the principle of matriliny, a specific matrilineage, learning, and the unity and persistence of Ndembu society (Turner, 1967, p. 28).

I invite you to reflect with me on one of the dominant ritual symbols in funerals in American society. The symbol of *body*.

The body is a very important symbol at death rituals for all societies. The physical facts of death make persons have to deal with the transformation from living body to dead body. This is a universal fact for all human societies. We have already mentioned that there is immense variability in the way different societies deal with this (Huntington and Metcalf, 1979).

A key to the understanding of what Americans do with dead bodies can be in exploring how the living body is regarded.

The human body is extremely important to Americans. At birth the body is washed, examined by a physician, and weighed. Washing, weighing, periodic physical examinations, and the beautifying of the body continue to be important throughout life. Young beautiful bodies are shown in the news media, and are used to sell products which will keep the body young and beautiful. Health and weight control is extremely important to Americans throughout life. There is a large concentration of energy, resources, and money allocated to health and weight control at the personal and societal levels. The number of books and programs related to diet and weight control are an indication of this. Moreover, Americans are exhorted (legally or morally) and exhort each other to have physical examinations not only at times of illness, but at the other key times of life transitions, like birth, infancy, pre-school at all levels, premarriage, before serving in the armed forces, and at death.

At the time of a death, it is not surprising that most Americans want to see the body cleaned and as life-like as possible for one last time. The transformation of the living body into a corpse must be horrifying to a people for whom "the body beautiful" is such an important symbol.

The Christian faith and the funeral introduces the symbol of the resurrected Body of Christ and the hope that all Christians will be resurrected with Christ. This adds meaningfulness to the symbol. It gives consolation to faithful Christians, but empirical Americans who have never seen or touched a resurrected body don't know what to expect and when. The very meaningfulness of the symbol increases the terror. How does one understand a body which cannot be weighed, washed, and made beautiful? The sensory body starts decaying immediately after death. The resurrected body is a symbol which requires a different dimension of understanding. The bereaved see themselves in between these two understandings, in a liminal place with regard to the symbol of the body.

A body at a funeral represents the symbol at the extreme end of its sensory pole.[5] The bereaved can see it and touch it. But what is being communicated when the body is not there? Is it an unwillingness to see and touch decay? When a bereaved person like Miss Strain says that she does not want to see her dead mother like "a painted doll," she may be evading decay, but she may also be reflecting the confusion and mystification which occurs in a liminal place.

However, it is important to note for the purposes of analysis of the dominant ritual symbol of body, that at a funeral the body is symbolically there even when it is not actually there. It is there even in its sensory pole because of the sensory meanings invested in the living body. Death means that the person can no longer be there in the same way. Because the dead person is there in a different way, the living are called to be there in a unique way. They are there because of the deceased; the deceased has called them to gather as community. They are usually all there: the lonely, the devastated, the indifferent, those who loved him, those who hated him, the curious ones, those only tangentially involved who only come because of duty. They are all called to *become One Body* for a short while. Each one has an opportunity to be transformed by the ritual.

At the other pole there is the way we talk about the word "body." "The legislative body," or the "body politic," the "body of the law," the "embodiment of high principles," the "body of a car," the "body of a written document." There are also the words of the Latin root *corps*. For example, Americans talk about being "corporate members," of "corporations," of the Marine "Corps," of the Army "Corps of Engineers." Even the word constitution has a corporeal meaning.

At every death ritual the participants receive large communications, verbal and non-verbal, of the symbol of body at all levels of meaning, from the sensory to the ideological pole. It is the bringing together of the sensory and ideological poles which makes the ritual powerful. It is not a matter of transcending the sensory through an ideological meaning or of the sensory meaning making the ideological more stark and present. It is both at once. It is at the moment of integration of the presence of those two poles of meaning in the ritual that spiritual presence is achieved. Community and communication become transformed into communion. Communion is the presence of all who have been part of the Body of Christ in the past, are a part of it now, and will become a part of it. Time is transcended and persons are transformed. This is what is possible at every death ritual.

Because of the convergence of meanings of the symbol during the ritual, it is possible that other meanings, even those which involve paradoxes can be heard, and, if not understood, can be apprehended and engaged. These are a few examples: Life is ended, yet life continues; persons die, yet new persons are created; death does not make sense, yet death is meaningful; humans are expendable, yet humans are precious; suffering is a fact of life, so is comfort; fear and horror are a part of human life, so are courage and beauty.

CONCLUSION

I sense that you know and are committed to the charges before you with regard to death rituals. Let me add a few to those. I speak as an immigrant nurse who has cared for and washed sick, dying, and dead bodies, as a Christian woman, and as an anthropologist who continues to observe and to participate in American ways, though at times with puzzlement.

1. It is more important to listen to a person and a community than to try to solve their problems, and especially to continue to do so, after the funeral. I know that some parish communities are providing ritual contact with families after funerals. I would affirm what you probably already know: that it is vital.

2. It is important to be aware of American values in our lives. While we want the Christian values of trusting God and our communities, we often prefer the American values of being individualistic, private, independent and in control. These values are not bad. We treasure them; they are valuable to us, but they are extremely hard to live up to, when our hearts are breaking, when there is violence, and when we are revolted by catastrophic events. That is where the Christian ritual can transform us right where we are. It can help us see our American values in the context of our Christian values. We cannot *just* be Roman Catholics, we have to be American Catholics. We have to be who we are.

3. I have a great concern related to another point, to which I referred earlier through the vignette. Namely our psychological-mindedness. This is an American tendency. Most educated Americans have heard about, and learned the stages of dying and grieving. Many pastoral persons have attended at least one workshop on death and dying. It is so tempting when one knows something intellectually to tell people what they ought to be feeling, instead of listening to what they actually are feeling. It is important to remember that listening is the primary attitude for prayer.

NOTES

1. Traditionally, there have been five distinct episodes in Catholic funeral rites:

   1) The body is carried to the church in doleful cortege of clergy and mourners with the intoning of psalms and the purificatory use of incense.
   2) The coffin is deposited in the church. The Office of the Dead is recited or sung: "Eternal rest grant unto him/her, O Lord! and let perpetual light shine upon him/her."
   3) The Requiem Mass is said or sung; sacrifice is offered for the repose of the soul.
   4) "Absolution" of the dead person, in which the coffin is solemnly perfumed with incense and sprinkled with holy water.
   5) The body is carried to consecrated ground and buried—appropriate prayers are recited by the officiating priest.

2. The new *Order of Christian Funerals* retains the basic theme of passage and includes several related rites and prayers: "Prayers after Death," "Gathering in the Presence of the Body," "Transfer of the Body to the Church or to the Place of Committal."

3. There is a recognizable trend toward choosing cremation, but I do not have any data measuring or analyzing the trend. It could be that cremation represents a further shortening of the funeral. Any analysis of what choosing cremation represents for the American people will have to take into consideration the symbolic meaning of body, as a dominant ritual symbol.

4. Among Puerto Ricans in Rochester, N.Y., there is a custom of nine nights of mourning by the entire community at the home of the deceased. The Rosary is prayed; there are prayers for the deceased and for the family. Food and money are shared. At the end of the nine nights there is often a Mass and an acknowledgement that this marks the end of the intensity of mourning. This seems to serve the function of a final death ritual for the participants. (I am indebted to Sr. Mary Regis, R.S.M., for our conversations about her work with Puerto Rican communities, and to Sr. Barbara Joan Lynaugh for our conversation about her ministry with funeral homes.)

5. When I was a young student nurse in Egypt, nurses were taught and expected to do what was known as post-mortem care. This was a

bath of the dead body right after death and a covering of all body orifices. I remember at times being horrified by my assignment. At other times, it was comforting to cry while I gave my patient his last bath. The memory of those times helped me to comprehend the importance of the sensory pole of meaning of the symbol of body.

REFERENCES

Apulius, *The Transformation of Lucius Otherwise Known as The Golden Ass.* Translated by R. Graves (1951). The Noon-day Press, A division of Farrar, Straus & Giroux, New York.

Bloch, M. and Parry, J. (eds.) (1983). *Death and the Regeneration of Life.* Cambridge and New York: Cambridge University Press.

Dempsey, D. (1975). *The Way We Die: An Investigation of Death and Dying in America Today.* New York: McGraw Hill.

Fortes, M. (1962). "Ritual and Office in Tribal Society." In *Essays on the Ritual of Social Relations.* Manchester University Press.

Geertz, C. (1973). *The Interpretation of Cultures.* New York: Basic Books, Inc.

Hamilton, C. and Osterdorf, L. (1963). *Lincoln in Photographs: An Album of Every Known Pose.* Norman: University of Oklahoma Press.

Huntington, R. and Metcalf, P. (1979). *Celebrations of Death: The Anthropology of Mortuary Ritual.* Cambridge and New York: Cambridge University Press.

Jackson, C. P. (ed.) (1977). *Passing: The Vision of Death in America.* Westport, Conn.: Greenwood Press.

Kalish, R. A. and Reynolds, D. K. (1976). *Death and Ethnicity: A Psychocultural Study.* Los Angeles: University of Southern California Press.

Kantorowicz, E. (1957). *The King's Two Bodies: A Study in Medieval Political Theory.* Princeton, N.J.: Princeton University Press.

Leach, E. R. (1961). Two essays concerning the symbolic representation of time. In *Rethinking Anthropology.* London: Althone Press.

Mack, A. (ed.) (1973). *Death in American Experience.* New York: Schocken.

Malinowski, B. (1948, 1954). *Magic, Science and Religion and Other Essays.* New York: Garden City.

Mitford, J. (1963). *The American Way of Death.* New York: Simon & Schuster.

Radcliff-Brown, A. R. (1965, 1952). *Structure and Function in Primitive Society.* New York: Free Press.

Rosenblatt, P. C., Walsh, R. P., and Jackson, D. A. (1976). *Grief and Mourning in Cross-Cultural Perspective.* Washington: Human Relations Area Files.

Smith, M. (1981, 1954). *Baba of Karo: A Woman of the Muslim Hausa.* New Haven and London: Yale University Press.

Stannard, D. (ed.) (1974). *Death in America.* University of Pennsylvania Press.

Sudnow, E. (1967). *Passing On: The Social Organization of Dying.* Englewood Cliffs, N.J.: Prentice-Hall, Inc.

Turner, V. (1967). *The Forest of Symbols.* Ithaca, N.Y.: Cornell University Press.

Turner, V. (1968). *The Drums of Affliction.* Oxford: The Clarendon Press.

VanGennep, A. *The Rites of Passage.* Translated by Vizedom, M. B. and Coffee, G. L. Chicago: The University of Chicago Press. 1909, 1960.

Zborowski, M. (1969). *People in Pain.* San Francisco: Jossey-Bass.

Funeral Liturgy—Why Bother?
A Practical Theology of Death
and Bereavement

H. RICHARD RUTHERFORD, C.S.C.

INTRODUCTION

*E*ven a casual glance at the obituaries of any daily newspaper demonstrates that for many in our society the answer
to "funeral liturgy—why bother?" is negative. Our peers in
the human and health sciences find this alarming. It strikes
you and me even more alarming to find an increasing number of active Catholics among those listings. Their choice
for "private interment" or even no funeral liturgy at all is
heralding a radical turning point in our liturgical tradition
and, I would suggest, in our Catholic faith as received and
professed by the Church in the United States.

Twenty years of research and writing on the liturgical
history and theology surrounding death among Christians
coupled with the challenges posed by my involvement in
the "Ritual-Language-Action" study group of the North
American Academy of Liturgy have led me to pose the practical theological question behind the scenes of our current
pastoral liturgical concerns. That is: What role does our
funeral liturgy play today in the experience of American
Catholics—especially those most immediately confronted
with death?

Inspired by Mark Searle's invitation to engage in multi-disciplinary dialogue in pastoral liturgical studies, as outlined in his vice-presidential address to the NAAL (1983), I have taken the liberty to apply the challenge of his proposal to quantitative research in service of pastoral practice. Thus, in a manner analogous to Searle's challenge, I would like to propose an answer to this present pastoral question based on the results of some initial empirical, hermeneutical, and critical analyses.

I wish to acknowledge my indebtedness to Dr. Harriet A. Kandelman, School of Business Administration, University of Portland. Her collegial assistance in the preparation and execution of our research as well as in the publication of the results of the study make it possible for me to carry out this pastoral liturgical analysis. All of us can be grateful for her contribution as research specialist; I alone can take credit for the technical limitations of my analyses.

I. EMPIRICAL RESEARCH

Ever since Eric Lindemann wrote his classic article on "Symptomatology and the Management of Acute Grief" (1944), much of bereavement literature has included religion as a variable in the study of bereavement, grief, and mourning. Although religion is widely acknowledged as a variable in the bereavement literature, the consensus, as summarized for example by Parkes and Weiss (1983), indicates that whether one is religious or non-religious does not significantly affect bereavement outcome. Yet, the question remains: What about those who are, in fact, religious? Does their religiosity play any role in their bereavement and mourning experience?

TABLE 0.1

Definition of Terms

BEREAVEMENT: the reaction to the loss of a close relationship, ordinarily found to express itself in some form of grief (Raphael, 1983).

GRIEF: the emotional response to loss, i.e., the complex amalgam of painful affects including sadness, anger, helplessness, guilt, despair (Raphael, 1983); not necessarily synonymous with bereavement (Fulton, 1965).

MOURNING: the psychological and symbolic processes that occur in bereavement, i.e., the process of grief work (Parkes, 1972); understood to include ritualized expressions of bereavement (Kastenbaum, 1981; Parkes, 1972).

BEREAVEMENT OUTCOME: the state of the survivor (bereaved) as the mourning processes end; measured by multivariate bio-psycho-social-spiritual indicators of reintegration to life without the deceased.

RELIGIOSITY: association with a Roman Catholic parish community whereby the subjects can be termed practicing Catholics, or spouses of Catholics, and have participated in the religious funeral services and pastoral care provided by the parish at the death of their spouses.

Acknowledging the multidimensional quality of religion and the extreme difficulty in measuring religiosity, this study follows the approach that defines religion in terms of both content and expression (including beliefs, attitudes, opinions, and behaviors). Furthermore, following E. Durkheim (1951) and more specifically Nelson and Cantrell (1980), our approach takes religious behavior as having a greater effect than religious belief on the management of emotions (e.g., reduction of anxiety about death). Thus, our empirical question can legitimately focus on one dimension of religious behavior, namely, the outward expression of religion in liturgy, specifically in Roman Catholic funeral rites where both content (religious belief) and expression (funeral liturgy) are operative.

Posed as a research question, it reads: Does the funeral liturgy function in a meaningful way in the bereavement experience of religious Catholics (specifically widowed persons, who as a group constitute a manageable population as well as one at high risk and thus deserving of our pastoral liturgical attention). Following standard social science methods for quantitative research, several sets of variables were established to measure the association between funeral rites and the bereavement experience.

TABLE 0.2

Areas about which Questions Were Asked by Questionnaire

Beliefs and Opinions of Survivors about Funeral Services and Pastoral Care	Table 1
Specific Rites of the Roman Catholic *Order of Christian Funerals*	Table 3
Demographics	Table 4
Attitudes and Behavior Patterns of Surviving Spouses	Table 5

Research data were provided by a nationwide study which sought responses to two questionnaires: one from parish clergy and the other from widowed persons. This paper deals mostly with responses from the widowed persons.

TABLE 4

DEMOGRAPHICS

AGE: Range 29–83 years ($\underline{M}$ = 61.3)   29-45: 17%
                                                    46-64: 37%
                                                    65-83: 46%

GENDER: Female 78%   Male 22%

RACE: Caucasian

GEOGRAPHY: Primarily small urban and rural with East and
Midwest most highly represented. Every
R.C. diocese except 8 (with 4 of those in
California).

OCCUPATION (Principal wage-earner before death):
            cross section

EDUCATION: High school diploma or less   61%
           Some college/college degree/higher   39%

RELIGION: Roman Catholic
          (principal sample)   88% ($\underline{N}$ = 36)
          Protestant
          (spouse of deceased Catholic) 12% ($\underline{N}$ = 5)

YEARS MARRIED: Range 6-59 years
               Less than 25 years: 25%
               26-51 years: 58%
               Longer than 51 years: 17%

HEALTH (self-appraisal):
               Excellent   24%
               Good   37%
               Average   32%
               Not so good   7%

CAUSE OF DEATH: Cancer   35%
                Heart   33%
                Stroke   12%
                Other (one of these, suicide) 20%

FOREWARNING: One month or less
                        54% (unanticipated)
             Longer than one month
                        46% (anticipated)

The sampling frame for this study was established from a list of widowed persons provided by pastors of five hundred randomly selected (using the *Official Catholic Directory*, 1982) Roman Catholic parishes throughout the United States, including Alaska and Hawaii. All fifty states and every Roman Catholic diocese, except eight (four in California), were represented in the initial five hundred parishes contacted.

Each pastor was provided with instructions guiding the choice of one widowed person from his parish. A profile described the desired subject in terms of religious practice, gender, month of the death, and a preferred time-frame of between thirteen and twenty-four months since the death of his or her spouse. Where this time-frame was impossible, the parish priest was authorized to extend it beyond twenty-four months but to remain as close as possible to the date of death, not to exceed four years.

Of the five hundred parishes selected and to whom questionnaires were mailed, 108 (22 percent) priests responded. Ninety-three priests agreed to participate; sixty-two participated fully by securing a widowed person who fit the profile and who agreed to complete a spouse questionnaire; the remaining thirty-one priest-respondents participated in part by returning a companion questionnaire for priests.

Only fifteen questionnaires were returned without responses, due to death of the addressee, illness, lack of time, etc. The sample established through the cooperation of these priests consisted of religious widowed persons whose spouses died between thirteen and twenty-four months, with only several extending to three or four years prior to being contacted for participation in this study. This time-frame was chosen to ensure that each subject would have lived through the experience of one or more years of widowhood, including significant anniversaries, but would still be close enough to the death to expect adequate recall of its impact (Parkes and Weiss, 1983). A total of sixty-two widowed persons responded (returning the questionnaires themselves by mail using the postage-paid envelope provided). Note: after the priest himself selected and invited the widow/widower to participate, the widowed person was on her/his own to carry through. Twenty-one of these fell outside the sample due to the rigor of selection, allowing a valid N of forty-one spouses.

To the lay person, used to large Gallup polls and the like, this seems a very small number. However, in accord with the assumptions of parametric statistics, these numbers are quite respectable, falling nicely in the range of "over 25, preferably 30 to less than 120" (Hays, 1963).

Limitations

We must always keep in mind the old saying about "lies, damn lies, and statistics." Statistics do not prove anything; they describe—in this case—the tiniest piece of a very complex human reality. Take all of this with a grain of salt, if you will, but remembering all the while that the "this" in question is something that has never been described before in the same manner. All the same, it is important to mention several limitations of the study that have bearing upon this pastoral liturgical analysis.

1. Because the widowed persons' priests were requested to establish the sampling frame, some selection and social desirability bias might be at work in subject responses, especially those that concern the clergy, such as availability, helpfulness, etc. To counter this each priest was provided

with a strict subject profile that would limit his choosing an ideal widowed person, as it were. Furthermore, the widowed subjects were invited to complete and return their personal questionnaires independent of their parish priests. Not only did about one-third of the priest respondents indicate that they were unable to find a widowed person who fit the profile, but also among the widowed participants identified, only those subjects were included by us in the sample who in fact fit the assigned profile. Taken together, these precautions will have preserved the sample from serious bias. Nevertheless, it seems inevitable that whatever selection bias did inadvertently occur would tend to impact such things as subjects' appraisal of clergy rather than other significant attitudes, beliefs, etc.

2. The choice to examine only religious Roman Catholic widowed persons is a limitation to generalizing the results for religions other than Roman Catholicism. This population was selected, however, to measure one of the most homogeneous experiences of religious funeral rituals available. Allowing for appropriate personalization in each specific case and for variations in ministerial style among the Catholic clergy, all the subjects will have experienced the same ritual patterns as specified in the *Rite of Funerals* (United States Catholic Conference, 1970). Thus, although the specific findings apply only to American Roman Catholic funerals (which in 1983, however, did, in fact represent approximately 420,000 among a Catholic population of nearly 52,400,000), the questions posed by the study now provide a research context for examining other religious funeral ritualization, especially in those Churches that share similar liturgical traditions with Roman Catholicism.

3. The retrospective nature of the study, with outcome measures and funeral experiences tested by subject self-rating and recall, was likewise tolerated as a place to break ground in this unique cross-disciplinary study between specifically liturgical theology and the behavioral sciences. Relying only on written questionnaires was deemed tolerable for the same reason. Nevertheless, a follow-up interview by telephone to subjects who authorized such a call on the questionnaire was planned, but postponed.

4. Also in need of greater sensitivity in the study are (a) the importance of forewarning of death, and (b) the survivors' personality traits, when treated as outcome determinants. Although these and other refinements indicate valuable directions in further work with this study and future research on the topic, they have not severely limited the value of the results for pastoral-liturgical theology.

Some Empirical Results

Indicators of bereavement recovery, together with religious attitudes and behavior patterns, were identified and examined in comparison with the widowed persons' recall of the impact of specific funeral rituals. Let us begin with data closest to the liturgy.

TABLE 1 presents items that tested selected beliefs and opinions of survivors about funeral services and pastoral availability at the time of the funeral and afterwards.

On a five-point scale [ranging from "extremely" to "not at all"] funeral rites, such as the Vigil for the Deceased, the Mass or Funeral Liturgy, Reception at the Church, were reported as extremely important to survivors in general (item 1; $\underline{M}$ = 4.63). Responding to a more specific question about their own experience our widowed persons reported funeral

TABLE 1

*Items Testing Beliefs and Opinions of Survivors
about Funeral Services and Pastoral Care*

1. Importance of mourning and grief rituals (e.g, wakes and funerals) for survivors
2. Value of prayers and Mass for the dead themselves
3. Importance of Catholic funeral services and Mass for the parish community
4. Effectiveness of the various religious services and funeral Mass in helping subjects with grief at the time of the death
5. Importance of memory of funeral services in helping subjects with grief since the funeral
6. Availability of parish priest(s) at the time of death and funeral
7. Attentiveness of parish priest(s) and others in helping plan the funeral
8. Availability of parish priest(s) after the funeral
9. Helpfulness of parish priest(s) availability
10. Overall satisfaction with funeral arrangements

rites to have been extremely effective in helping them deal with their grief at the time of their partner's death (item 4; M = 4.65). Finally, the memory of the funeral services they experienced was reported by our widowed persons to have been extremely important to themselves in the time since the funeral (item 5; M = 4.37). These findings, already interesting in themselves, become more valuable when looked at in relation to each other. What association exists between our subjects' general opinion about the value of funeral rites and more specific recollections of their own bereavement?

TABLE 1.1

*Correlation for Subject Response to Beliefs and Opinion
about Funeral Services and Pastoral Care*

1. Importance of mourning and grief rituals   r =   .34
   (e.g., wakes and funerals) for survivors   p < .05
   ($\underline{M}$ = 4.63, $\underline{N}$ = 40) r^2 =   .12

5. Importance of memory of religious funeral
   services in helping subjects with grief in the
   time since the funeral ($\underline{M}$ = 4.37, $\underline{N}$ = 41)

4. Effectiveness of the various religious ser-   r =   .78
   vices and funeral Mass in helping subjects   p < .001
   with grief at the time of the death r^2 =   .61
   ($\underline{M}$ = 4.65, $\underline{N}$ = 40)

5. Importance of memory of religious funeral
   services in helping subjects with grief in
   the time since the funeral

   ****

1. Importance of mourning and grief rituals   NS
   (e.g., wakes and funerals) for survivors
4. Effectiveness of the various religious services and funeral Mass in helping subjects
   with grief at the time of death

Comparing the report that the memory of the funeral liturgy helped our subjects deal with their grief in the time since the funeral (item 5) with their opinion of the general importance of the rituals for survivors (item 1) showed a low to moderate correlation (item 5 with 1; r = .34). That is, according to this sample, knowing that our subjects have a high regard for grief rituals in general, there is about a one in three chance of anticipating correctly that their memory of what happens in the funeral liturgy will be helpful in their time of grieving. Furthermore, the importance of this memory (item 5) was highly correlated with their estimation of the effectiveness of the funeral liturgy in helping our subjects deal with their grief at the time of the death (item 5 with 4; r = .78). This result shows that in our sample finding the funeral liturgy helpful in their grief at the time of the loss suggests a high likelihood that remembering their partner's funeral was also helpful in the longer span of their bereavement. One further comparison between the widowed persons' general opinion about the value of grief rituals (item 1) and this belief about the effectiveness of the funeral liturgy in their own bereavement (item 4) reveals no statistically significant correlation. In other words, they are independent: our subjects' opinion about the effectiveness of the funeral liturgy in their grief at the time of death is not influenced by their belief about the value of grief rituals in general. Neither does this general opinion contribute to the correlation between items 4 and 5. We shall have occasion below to discuss further the importance of this finding about the role that remembering the funeral liturgy plays in bereavement outcome.

A second noteworthy result of our empirical analysis concerns the community ministry of the Church, a major focus and principal contribution of the *Order of Christian Funerals.* One of the more significant dimensions contributing to favorable bereavement outcome is an appropriate social support system. Support from those who share the same religious beliefs and rituals, especially from priests and other ministers of the Catholic community, has been identified as part of the broader social support network.

When asked about the importance of funeral liturgy for the parish community as a whole, our subjects responded in the same fashion as above: extremely important (item 3; $\underline{M}$ = 4.39). Similarly, there is a statistically significant (low to moderate) correlation between this community consciousness and their general opinion about the value of funeral liturgy (item 1; r = .49). It is curious to note, however, that the correlation between our subjects' view of the importance of funeral liturgy to the community (item 3) and the demographic report about the number of years they had been married at the time of their spouses' death reveals a low-level likelihood that the longer subjects were married, the less they would be inclined to describe funeral liturgy as important to the parish community as a whole.

When it comes to rating the role clergy and other ministers play in this social support network, generally speaking bereavement studies have not found Catholic clergy to receive very complimentary grades. This study, on the contrary, found religious widowed parishioners rating their clergy extremely supportive, and the clergy consistently cited their personal presence to the bereaved as a major pastoral priority.

The availability of priests and other ministers at the time of the death and funeral (item 6), as well as after the funeral (item 8) received high scores by our subjects. Furthermore, almost nine out of ten (88 percent) reported such availability at those times (item 9) to have been helpful, very helpful or extremely helpful. Both parish priests and widowed parishioners agreed that the priest's being available was helpful.

TABLE 1

*Items Testing Beliefs and Opinions of Survivors
about Funeral Services and Pastoral Care*

1. Importance of mourning and grief rituals (e.g, wakes and funerals) for survivors
2. Value of prayers and Mass for the dead themselves
3. Importance of Catholic funeral services and Mass for the parish community
4. Effectiveness of the various religious services and funeral Mass in helping subjects with grief at the time of the death
5. Importance of memory of funeral services in helping subjects with grief since the funeral
6. Availability of parish priest(s) at the time of death and funeral
7. Attentiveness of parish priest(s) and others in helping plan the funeral
8. Availability of parish priest(s) after the funeral
9. Helpfulness of parish priest(s) availability
10. Overall satisfaction with funeral arrangements

The low to moderate, yet statistically significant, correlation found between both clergy availability at the time of death (item 6) with availability after the funeral (item 8), and with subjects' appraisal of clergy helpfulness (item 9), affirm these findings. Clergy availability at the death and funeral (item 6) revealed an equally strong correlation with their attentiveness toward planning the funeral (item 7). Thus, in this religious sample, priests and other ministers were more likely to be considered helpful when their availability at death included an attentiveness toward planning and also extended to the time after the funeral.

TABLE 2

Correlation for Subject Response to Availability, Attentiveness and Helpfulness of Priests before and after the Funeral

	7	8	9
6	.29*	.39**	.28*
7		.52***	.62***
8			.72***

Note: All significance levels are one-tailed.

    p < .05

   **p* < .01

  ***p* < .001

This latter facet corresponds closely with the finding of Carey (1979–1980) that follow-up visits by clergy, although rare, were greatly appreciated. In fact, the far stronger correlations between subjects' appraisal of clergy helpfulness (item 9) and both clergy attentiveness at funeral planning (item 7; r = .62) and their availability after the funeral (item 8; r = .72) confirmed the accuracy of that impression. Similarly, the data showed a strong tendency for priests who are attentive at planning (item 7) also to be available after the funeral (item 8; r = .52).

Yet, when parallel questions asked of the parish priests who participated in the study (i.e., the priests who cared for the same funerals reported by the widowed persons) were analysed, it is surely not a coincidence that the same combinations of data likewise revealed statistically significant correlations. Rather, it is a further confirmation that this particular matter of pastoral care is quite important to both clergy and widowed persons in our sample. These results point up further that where the widowed persons seem to place a slightly greater emphasis on pastoral availability after the funeral in weighing clergy support, the clergy themselves give greater weight to their availability at the time of death and funeral. This certainly corresponds to our ordinary experience. It both affirms our pastoral care before and during the time of the death and urges us to extend that care into the longer time of bereavement after the funeral.

In any case, it is fairly clear that both spouse and clergy appraisal of pastoral care at death depends significantly on the quality and extent of ministerial availability and attentiveness. In a similar way our data revealed a significant, albeit lower correlation between our widowed persons' appraisal of the helpfulness of ministerial availability (item 9) and their overall satisfaction with the funeral (item 10; r = .29). These findings support the importance of continuity in pastoral care surrounding the death of a parishioner and indicate the role lay bereavement ministers might play in enabling such continuity. It also corresponds with the results reported as early as 1967 by Maddison and Walker who showed the association between bereavement outcome and the quality and extent of environmental support generally, including interchanges of a religious nature. More recently Davidowitz and Myrick (1984) found that religious statements made to the bereaved ranked as high or low in facilitating breavement outcome, depending on the quality of the exchange, rather than on religious content as such.

An Empirical Conclusion

Both the funeral liturgy as a whole, as illustrated above, and specific rites of the *Order of Christian Funerals*, still to follow, were reported by the widowed spouses to serve several important functions in their bereavement. In the opinion of this sample, the funeral liturgy celebrated at the death of their spouses was effective in their initial expression of reaction to the loss and continued to play an effective role in the longer span of their mourning. Empirically one can affirm, therefore, that for this sample funeral rites contributed in a meaningful way to their bereavement outcome.

II. HERMENEUTICAL MUSINGS

Foundational to the hermeneutical task, whether seeking to understand measurable meaning or the thick description of the ethnographer, are two questions: What is meant? and, How does meaning happen? While I do not yet have an adequate answer to these questions for the funeral liturgy, I have a suspicion—an hermeneutical intuition almost—that an answer will have something to do with what we traditionally called "the consolation of the faith." By this phrase I do not imply the "opiate theory" whereby one's religious beliefs are thought to deaden an integrated participation in the bereavement experience. Rather the results of our empirical research are leading me to affirm the exact opposite position, that is: full, active and conscious participation in our Roman Catholic faith in both belief and behavior, especially as those take symbolic expression in the funeral liturgy, is an inherently therapeutic experience which—from inside out as it were— enables healthy, normal bereavement. In this section of the paper therefore I would like to review with you some "ground breaking" for the larger hermeneutical task of discerning the "what" and the "how" of meaning in the celebration of the *Order of Christian Funerals.*

Remembering

Our study has demonstrated that a strong association exists between the memory of the funeral liturgy experienced at the time of the death and the perception that such a memory was helpful during bereavement. Analysis of responses having to do with survivors' memory of the liturgy, their general opinion about the importance of such rites, and their effectiveness at the time of their spouses' death shows clearly that it was the memory of the funeral liturgy as meaningful and effective at the time of their partners' death that played a role in their mourning during the time since the death. Remembering will thus surely have some role to play in "how" funeral rites are effective in bereavement. Although not treated as part of this study, each and every parish funeral plays a role in the collective remembering of the community which, as every student of ritual here knows so well, is precisely the framework within which any specific funeral will be remembered. Let us examine our data with this thesis in mind.

Selected Rites of the **Order of Christian Funerals**

In the liturgical time between death and the funeral liturgy in the church (assuming the ordinary practice still current in the United States) many of the recommended occasions for prayer are indeed represented in the pastoral practice experienced by our subjects. For example, the desire of the liturgical renewal to instill a greater biblical spirit appears to be taking hold. Both spouses and priests indicated widespread recollection of the Bible vigil as the most frequently celebrated service before the funeral liturgy. It is interesting, however, that parish priests cited the vigil 20 percent more often than did the widowed persons. It might be that we are witnessing a language or communication discrepancy in these reports. Nevertheless, the vigil with the deceased has caught on and is being remembered as part of Catholic funeral liturgy by our spouse subjects as well as by the clergy.

This is not to say that the vigil is thereby completely replacing the Rosary. On the contrary, our study shows that the Rosary has retained much of its popularity, with 40 percent of our subjects reporting both vigil and the Rosary. Most recalled both services in the same location. Twenty percent of those reporting different locations for the vigil and the Rosary recalled the vigil in church and the Rosary in the funeral home. What seems to be taking place is the introduction of the new "vigil for the deceased" as the principal liturgical celebration and the continuation of the Rosary as the popular prayer form offered by parish groups such as the Altar and Rosary Society or Knights of Columbus when they gather for condolences. This study thus reveals a "both-and" description (Bible vigil and the Rosary) which likewise seems to be happening organically and without articulated objections, at least not among our sample. To the extent that this sample is representative of the population studied we might well be witnessing an ideal solution. In this way memory is being engaged in renewed biblical images and familiar popular religious practices.

Other than the "vigil for the deceased" and its counterpart, the traditional Rosary, two occasions for prayer during this time before the funeral liturgy received frequent mention among our widowed persons. Almost half (46 percent) of our subjects recalled prayers when they first saw the deceased and 66 percent remembered prayers at the closing of the casket. Although nearly one-third (30 percent) of the priests also report those times for prayer as general practice in their parishes, those services seem more memorable still to the widowed persons themselves. Mass with the family during this time, although not noted in the recommendations of the *Rite of Funerals* (1970), is reported as common practice in the experience of almost one-third of our widowed persons and over 25 percent of the parish priests surveyed.

The special attention devoted to such services between death and the funeral liturgy in the church in the *Order of Christian Funerals* provides a much needed model for clergy and lay ministers to be present to bereaved parishioners at times they themselves have identified as most difficult. Those rites and the prayers provided in appendices of the *Order* will also assist parish ministers with the preparation of post-funeral rites, an area of liturgical pastoral care which, as you recall, both spouse and clergy subjects reported to be important and deserving of attention.

In this vein the traditional, albeit currently less familiar, Catholic practice of celebrating a memorial of the death at one month, the "month's mind," is an example of an occasion that allows a continued contact between parish ministers and bereaved parishioners. When asked about this practice, less than one-third of our subjects stated (not unexpectedly) that such a month's memorial was available. Yet, where available, all but one of those widowed persons attended the service. Further analysis revealed that in over half the cases where parishioners stated that the month's memorial was available, the clergy reported that the practice was not available. This confirms all the more strongly that for the bereaved, holding a first month's memorial (possibly simply the matter of requesting that Mass be celebrated) was significant. Among those subjects who were not aware of the memorial at the first month or where the custom was not current, 91 percent indicated that they would have found such an opportunity helpful. Our sample of actively religious widowed parishioners affirms the importance of post-funeral ritualization as one dimension at least of pastoral care in the wake of death and burial. Not only does such a practice engage the memory of the bereaved in the faith of the Church expressed liturgically; it likewise engages the faith memory of the larger worshiping community that gathers for commemorative liturgies. Maintaining or revitalizing in contemporary form practices such as the historically traditional anniversaries of death (one month, one year) is recommended by this study.

Up to this point our hermeneutical "ground breaking" has examined rites before and after the Funeral Liturgy and the Rite of Committal. Let us now examine some results of our study pertaining to specific components of these two principal parts of the *Order of Christian Funerals.*

To guide this discussion we pose the following question. If our widowed subjects have shown that the funeral rites celebrated for their deceased spouses played a role in their bereavement experience both at the time of the death and afterwards, then what role did they play? Two functions were identified by the questionnaire to initiate an answer: Did the widowed spouses find the services to be comforting to themselves, and did they believe the services to be spiritually helpful to the deceased? Their responses to these questions for specific parts of the funeral liturgy led to the

TABLE 5*

*Items Testing Attitudes and Behavior Patterns
of Surviving Spouse*

1. If you visit your spouse's grave or resting place, how meaningful are such visits to you?
2. Have you given away most of your spouse's personal effects?
3. Has the death of your spouse resulted in financial hardship for you?
4. How would you describe the time of your mourning or grieving?
5. How would you describe your general health at the present time?
6. How would you describe your general health before your spouse's death?
7. How frequently do you see your friends since your spouse's death?
8. Have you made new friends since your spouse's death?
9. How patient do you find yourself with family and friends since your spouse's death?
10. How frequently do you get out of the house since your spouse's death?
11. Are you now living a life that is comfortable to you?

*See also Table 1

formation of two pairs of groups. One pair was the "comforting = yes" — "comforting = no" respondents; the other was the "spiritually helpful = yes" — "spiritually helpful = no" group. Further, two sets of indicators of the survivors' bereavement experience were identified. One of these measured patterns of life without the deceased (TABLE 5); the other, which we already used above, treats beliefs and opinions about funeral rites and pastoral care at the death of a loved one (TABLE 1).

Our findings confirm the experience of parish ministers that specific funeral rites contribute in different ways to the total impact of religion at the time of death. Yet we also begin to identify some trends that can help recognize the impact of specific rites on persons with some characteristic attitudes, behaviors, and beliefs.

Our widowed persons fell almost evenly into these two "Yes" and "No" groups. The task is not to examine the reasons why individual spouses responded as they did. Rather, we are interested to know whether their aggregate response about liturgical rites made any difference between the groups with reference to practical areas of pastoral care and bereavement outcome (TABLES 1 and 5). In other words, did a "Yes" or "No" answer about liturgy make any difference in the way our widowed persons responded to questions about pastoral care or their recovery from grief? The answer is, "Yes!" Their interpretation of funeral rites made a difference. "So what?" You are perhaps saying to yourselves, "We liturgists knew that all along!" That's the good news. The better news, and my answer to our liturgical "So what?" is that the specifics go on to help us better understand how the components of the funeral liturgy function in these two areas of human comfort in face of loss and a spirituality vis-à-vis the dead.

Caveat. Although this study has determined that these two ways of experiencing funeral rites make a difference, the impact of such a difference is only one, very minor factor among the many factors accounting for our widowed persons' opinions and beliefs about pastoral care and their bereavement outcome. This is not surprising in so complex

TABLE 3.1*

FUNERAL RITES

WIDOWED PERSONS FOUND CATHOLIC
FUNERAL RITES "SPIRITUALLY
HELPFUL" TO THE DEAD

YES	NO	
Value of prayer for the dead? (.06)	*Given away personal effects? (.06)* *Time of mourning? (.08)*	SPRINKLING CASKET WITH HOLY WATER
	Given away personal effects? (.06) *Time of mourning? (.08)*	SPREADING WHITE PALL OVER CASKET
	Given away personal effects? (.06) *Time of mourning? (.13)*	PASCHAL CANDLE WITH CASKET
Value of prayer for the dead? (.09)	*Given away personal effects? (.09)* *Time of mourning? (.06)*	FINAL COMMENDATION
Value of prayer for the dead? (.06)		EXIT PROCESSION WITH CASKET
Value of prayer for the dead? (.05)	Attentive help in planning the funeral (.11)	FINAL DISPOSITION (COMMITAL)

*See also Table 5.

a human phenomenon as loss and bereavement. It is all the more remarkable to discover that these liturgical rites make any measurable difference at all. Some examples touching several summary beliefs and opinions will suffice for the purposes of this presentation.

For example, survivors who do not report that they find the rituals of sprinkling holy water, spreading the white pall, placing the paschal candle, and the final commendation to be "spiritually helpful" to the deceased reveal a slight edge over those who do find these rites spiritually helpful to the dead loved one in relation to two summary items of healthy bereavement recovery (TABLE 5, items 2 and 4). Although the impact of the difference between the two groups is small and indicates that one ought not exaggerate the distinction, the impact that does exist seems to identify the "no" group as more likely than the "yes" group to report healthy bereavement responses (such as appropriately disposing of the deceased's personal belongings and perceiving oneself to be on the road to recovery).

The rituals of the Reception of the Body and the Introductory Rites of the Funeral Mass and the Final Commendation are related historically to holy water, purification, and blessing—all expressions of a belief that associated these rituals with spiritual value to the deceased. Yet, the "spiritually helpful = no" group shows higher mean scores on these rituals vis-à-vis healthy bereavement. Perhaps this reflects the distinction current in Catholic experience between an earlier emphasis on performing rituals of blessing and purification to assist the dead, where one might expect the "yes" group to have higher scores (cf. TABLE 3.1), and the contemporary theological emphasis that views the Easter mystery of the death and resurrection of the Lord rather than purification as the source of Christian hope for the deceased. In any case there is a statistically significant difference revealed in our results. To the extent that this sample is representative of the population, it would behoove us to take its indications seriously when planning and celebrating these rites with persons of such divergent faith memories.

One finding in particular illustrates how reporting a ritual to be comforting is related in the two groups (see TABLE 3.2). When one recognizes the dimension of psychological closure potentially operative in the exit procession with the casket from the church and committal on the one hand and disposing of the deceased's personal effects (TABLE 5, item 2) on the other, it is understandable that the group finding the solemn departure from the church and the committal rites comforting would very likely also report having cared for the deceased spouse's belongings by the time they participated in this study. Yet, what our results are showing is precisely that how they answer the "comforting" question with reference to the Exit and Committal makes a difference. The impact of that difference is seen to be quite small (omega squared = .08), but nevertheless we know something we did not know before. Here again one notes an indication of new pastoral care insights that can be helpful when planning the funeral or visiting widowed parishioners after the funeral.

Finally, results from studying our two sets of groups in relation to the other set of indicators (TABLE 1) support the findings noted above.

Among the "comforting" groups, for example, the importance of the memory of funeral rites (item 5) showed statistically significant differences between "yes" and "no" groups for four specific ritual actions: sprinkling, spreading the white pall, final commendation, and the exit from the

church with the casket. Thus in this sample, subjects reporting these specific rites to have been comforting to them
are more likely than those who answered not comforting
to have found the memory of the funeral helpful in their
bereavement.

Since it seems from this that ritual actions which are
perceived as comforting at the time of the death and funeral
are the ones to engage the memory of the bereaved (quite
likely the larger community as well) and thus facilitate
healthy bereavement, attending to what enables them to be
comforting becomes pastorally important. The four rites
where this difference appeared with statistical significance
for our sample perhaps point us in a direction. It might well
be that the very nature of human ritualization is the link
to remembering these rites as comforting and thus effective for bereavement. Religious ritual, like all ritual action,
functions at its optimum when it engages the religious imagi-
nation (Power, 1984; Collins, 1983). All four of the rites in
question are high-intensity ritual actions with religious symbols (water, pall, incense, movement) that involve the focal
symbol of the funeral (the casket) and touch the senses of
the participants. The two older, more traditional rites (Sprinkling at the Entrance and the Final Commendation with Incense) revealed a slightly stronger impact of the difference
(between the yes group and no group) on the memory question. The Exit with the Casket ranked next in impact, and
the newest of the rites (Spreading the Pall) ranked least, although the difference in ranking is so slight that it would
be splitting hairs to give any weight to this point. Arguing
from the failure to achieve statistical significance is, of course,
inappropriate. Yet one can't help but wonder why the liturgical role of the paschal candle or the Rite of Committal

TABLE 3.2*

FUNERAL RITES

WIDOWED PERSONS FOUND CATHOLIC
FUNERAL RITES "COMFORTING"
TO THEMSELVES

	YES	_NO_
SPRINKLING CASKET WITH HOLY WATER	Memory? (.07) Satisfaction? (.13)	
SPREADING WHITE PALL OVER CASKET	Memory? (.05) Satisfaction? (.08)	
PASCHAL CANDLE WITH CASKET	Satisfaction? (.07)	
FINAL COMMENDATION	Memory? (.07) Satisfaction? (.13)	
EXIT PROCESSION WITH CASKET	Memory? (.06) _Given away personal effects? (.08)_ _Grave visits? (.06)_ Satisfaction? (.07)	
FINAL DISPOSITION (COMMITAL)	_Given away personal effects? (.04)_ Satisfaction? (.15)	

*See also table 5.

would not also be ritual actions where subjects' report of "comforting" or "not comforting" would have a statistically significant impact on their response to the memory question. However that may be, TABLE 3.2 shows that all six of these ritual actions do have such a statistically significant impact on the subjects' overall satisfaction with the funeral of their deceased spouses! Here too the Sprinkling and the Final Commendation, but now also including the Committal, show the strongest impact. The measure of that impact (omega squared) in all three cases is nearly twice as great in the matter of overall satisfaction with the funeral as in that of remembering the rites.

The groups reporting these funeral rites as "spiritually helpful" to the deceased reveal that with reference to the Rite of Committal in the cemetery their answer shows a statistically significant difference when coupled with the matter of clergy attentiveness at helping plan the funeral (TABLE 1, item 7; cf. TABLE 3.1). In this case the NO group predominated. This result suggests a possible explanation of why helpfulness with planning is important to survivors. When Catholic funeral rituals in themselves are believed to be spiritually helpful to the deceased, proper execution alone of the ritual is sufficient to achieve the desired goal. When that is not the case, as indicated by the predominance of the "spiritually helpful = no" group in this finding, then the attentiveness of those responsible for effective ritual expression becomes important enough to impact the grief experience of survivors.

An Hermeneutical Conclusion

Roman Catholic faith and liturgy offer an interpretation of death and loss that is understandable and suggests a way of making sense out of the often incomprehensible mystery of death. Inseparably associated with such faith is the liturgy whereby the faith expresses itself in ritual form. Together these elements of Catholic religiousness embrace both the attitudinal and behavioral categories within which fall the many diverse dimensions of the concept religiosity. It is the contention of this study that Roman Catholic faith and practice, and in particular liturgical practice, offer to religious Catholics both the kind of belief system and the coping styles that can enhance recovery from bereavement. Where religious faith and practice have played an active and positive role in prebereavement beliefs and behaviors as well as at the time of the death and funeral, this study has determined that religious funeral rituals associate positively with healthy recovery from bereavement. It has shown further that specific rituals of the funeral liturgy may function differently in the grieving experience of divergent survivors. Differences were seen to depend on the expectations and faith perspectives of the bereaved coupled with the pastoral care accorded them at the time of the death and funeral as well as in the weeks and months thereafter.

III. CRITICAL IMPLICATIONS

Finally, using our empirical research and hermeneutical intuitions, what can be said in answer to the "Why bother?" attitude gradually infiltrating American Catholic funerary practice? First, we have discovered a strong affirmation in favor of traditional Catholic funeral rites and pastoral care. There is a high level of satisfaction on the part of the bereaved widowed persons of our sample toward the clergy and other parish ministers who attended them in their crisis.

Second, existing funeral rites, restored and renewed in light of the tradition, are seen to make a difference in the bereavement experience of our people. One can only expect that these rites will serve our people even better according to the revised edition of the *Order of Christian Funerals.*

Some concerns have also surfaced. First among those is our tendency to put too many eggs in too small a basket, as it were. We tend to focus most, if not all, of our pastoral attention on the vigil and funeral itself, and much less attention, if any at all, to the longer time-frame of the typical bereavement experience. Similarly, all of our attention seems to be devoted to the immediately bereaved. While they are, indeed, a primary focus of pastoral care at the time of death touching their lives, our analyses reveal the importance of refocusing some of that attention, at least, to the larger worshipping community of the Church. We have learned from our comparison of this study with the longer tradition that the funeral, as all liturgy, both expresses and impresses— signs and effects— the faith of the Church.

Next, there is a changing spirituality taking place among our people. The centrality of the Paschal Mystery in Catholic liturgical teaching and practice after the Second Vatican Council has begun to have its effect on the interpretation of funeral liturgy. Perhaps we are experiencing the fruit of the reformed funeral liturgy shaping our people. We saw, for example, that, while our sample affirmed with extreme confidence the value of prayer and Mass for the dead, about half of our subjects regularly demonstrated that in fact this principle played little or no role in practice when asked of specific rites. Furthermore, their position on this matter of belief made a difference with reference to attitudes and opinions about their bereavement and pastoral care. To what extent are our people now shaping funeral liturgy? To what extent are we attending to this changing spirituality when planning the funeral and following up after the funeral during bereavement? On the other end of the spectrum, there are those whose spirituality preserves earlier historical expressions of belief and ritual practice. Thus, with the changing spirituality, we must also recognize an increasing plurality of belief and expression, including many attendant ramifications for bereavement ministry.

A final concern would have to be the increasingly diminished role of the place of the church and the Catholic cemetery in the experience of this sample. Although we did not treat these two points specifically in this paper, our sample indicates that, while they affirm the pastoral care received from the clergy, they ultimately consider the clergy and the Church in the service of the funeral director. The same seems to apply to the Catholic cemetery. One would not be very far off the mark to say that even this highly religious and obviously liturgically engaged sample would find no contradiction between that profile and the typical funerary trappings of the secular mortuary and the one-stop funeral malls now marketed by the growing mortuary-cemetery industry. In other words, we must be critically aware that while our funeral rites constitute a significant value in the bereavement experience in this sample, it does not necessarily mean that such a value is universally perceived or could not give way to still other culturally and financially attractive options. In like manner, this paper reflects its sample's low profile regarding cremation, but in the three years since this data was first collected cremation has become one of the major pastoral liturgical issues in bereavement ministry. An increasing number of our people

will continue to affirm with those of this sample that Catholic
funeral rites are important to them and effective in their
bereavement and at the same time select immediate disposal
with a commercial cremation agency and show up on our
doorsteps with cremains in hand. What's left by way of
funeral liturgy? The so-called "memorial Mass." Is that single, ritual celebration really able to replace the broader
potential for organic healing available in the traditional rites?
As I have written elsewhere, cremation as a means of final
disposition can and will have its appropriate place in Catholic
funeral practice. I do believe, however, that our liturgical
tradition with its richly human attention to the body of the
deceased should guide our approach to developing such appropriate liturgical practice rather than the opposite trends
of the latest addition to the commercial funeral industry:
imemdiate disposal services. The *Order of Christian Funerals* offers models for us to work toward funeral liturgy with
cremation, and liturgically formed funeral directors are
providing appropriate "cremation caskets" with exterior cas-
ing that may be rented. All of this will take time, but then
again, so does the birth of all new symbols.

To the extent that pastoral practitioners fail to appre-
ciate Catholic funeral liturgy as counter-cultural, we could
surely see an increased move away from the central place
of the Church in the death and bereavement of our people,
and our liturgical expression of the Paschal Mystery in
funeral rites becoming one more reflection of the death-
denying dimensions of our culture. Happily, there are signs
that the prophetic voice of American Catholics in this matter are having an effect. The revised *Order of Catholic
Funerals* is certainly one of those, and its impact is already
a significant factor. A firm stand on asserting authentic litur-

gical expression of the Paschal Mystery and other Gospel values of the Catholic tradition in face of the cremation explosion is another. My point is simply that our empirical and hermeneutical analyses give us as much cause for continued awareness as for rejoicing.

Some Practical Conclusions for Action

As a basic perspective, think always of the *Order of Christian Funerals* and pastoral care to the bereaved in continuity. This would apply in pastoral practice and in the education of diocesan and parish bereavement ministers. All would come to recognize the larger context in which death occurs, including all three time-frames designated by the *Order of Christian Funerals*: the time between death and the Funeral Liturgy; the Funeral Liturgy itself (principally in the church); and finally, the time after that Funeral Liturgy, commencing with the Rite of Committal and continuing on throughout the bereavement experience. This continuity would apply in all bereavement thinking, including the liturgical treatment of cremation. Such a pastoral education would also include pre-planning both funeral and cemetery needs as a general practice. This would help a great deal to express the appropriate place of the parish church and the local Catholic cemetery in our care of the dead and bereaved, whatever the nature of the death, manner of final disposition and the like.

Second, think of the *Order of Christian Funerals* as a model liturgy enshrining the tradition and awaiting the breath of life anew rather than as a cookbook full of recipes. This attitude would apply at the time of a death but also for those times and rites not provided in the *Order* itself.

Finally, think "Church," that is, think ecclesially rather than exclusively family, bereaved, etc.

How to put this thinking into action? Among other things, where they do not yet exist, create, or, where they do, support and animate lay ministry teams to attend the dying and the bereaved. They serve to make the Church present throughout the long-run experience and provide ecclesial context for the specifically presbyteral presence. Such lay-ministry teams would, of course, be formed to know and use the liturgy and not, as is unfortunately sometimes still the case, only bio-psycho-social values exclusive of the liturgy. Another practical group or individual to be engaged or, where already existing, supported is, of course, the funeral choir or schola or at least, the funeral cantor. Next, take time to study the *Order of Christian Funerals* itself very well and teach it, through your lay ministry teams, to the entire parish community. Finally, do everything you can to make the church complex and the Catholic cemetery taken together—viewed as the single entity they once were—to be the center for the Roman Catholic funeral liturgy.

Indeed, this continues to be a very large agenda whose import is truly heralded by the anticipated publication of the *Order of Christian Funerals.* My desire in this paper has been to affirm, together with all the anonymous widowed persons and parish priests of this reseach study, that it is worth the effort. As the timely choice of this topic for the 1987 national meeting of the FDLC itself proclaims, funeral liturgy is worth the bother!

REFERENCES

1. Carey, R. G. (1979–1980). "Weathering widowhood: Problems and adjustments of the widowed during the first year." *Omega* 10, 163-74.
2. Davidowitz, M., and Myrick, R. D. (1984). "Responding to the bereaved: An analysis of 'helping' statements." *Death Education* 8, 1-10.
3. Durkheim, E. (1951). *Suicide*. (J. A. Spaulding & G. Simpson, trans.). New York: Free Press.
4. Hays, W. L. (1963). *Statistics for Psychologists*. New York: Holt, Rinehart and Winston.
5. Lindemann, E. (1944). "Symptomatology and management of acute grief." *American Journal of Psychiatry* 101, 141-48.
6. Maddison, D., and Walker, W. (1967). "Factors affecting the outcome of conjugal bereavement." *British Journal of Psychiatry* 113, 1057-67.
7. Nelson, L. D., and Cantrell, C.H. (1980). "Religiosity and death anxiety: A multi-dimensional analysis." *Review of Religious Research* 21, 148-57.
8. *Order of Christian Funerals*. Washington: International Commission on English in the Liturgy, Inc. 1985.
9. Parkes, C. M., and Weiss, R. S. (1983). *Recovery from Bereavement*. New York: Basic Books.
10. Power, David N. (1984). *Unsearchable Riches: The Symbolic Nature of Liturgy*. New York: Pueblo.
11. Raphael, B. (1983). *The Anatomy of Bereavement*. New York: Basic Books.
12. *Rite of Funerals*. Washington: United States Catholic Conference, 1970.
13. Rutherford, R., and Kandelman, H. (1985). "The Role of Religion in Spousal Bereavement: Roman Catholic Funeral Rituals. *Research Record: National Research and Information Center*, 2.
14. Searle, Mark. "New Tasks, New Methods: The Emergence of Pastoral Liturgical Studies." *Worship* 57 (1983) 291-308.

Contributors

LAWRENCE BOADT, C.S.P., is a professor of biblical studies at Washington Theological Union, Washington, D.C. He is the author of several books, including *Ezekiel's Oracles Against Egypt* and a commentary on the Book of Proverbs for the *Collegeville Bible Commentary* published by The Liturgical Press. He is a member of the Advisory Committee of the International Commission on English in the Liturgy and assisted with the *Order of Christian Funerals*.

MARY DOMBECK is a senior associate in nursing at the University of Rochester School of Nursing and serves as an associate counselor at the Samaritan Pastoral Counseling Center in Rochester, N.Y. She has presented workshops on depression in women, explanations of human suffering, dream groups, modeling listening skills, and principles for group process.

H. RICHARD RUTHERFORD, C.S.C.., is the chairman of the department of theology at the University of Portland, Oregon, and a member of the archdiocese of Portland liturgical commission. He is a specialist in the study of the role that liturgy and the sacraments play in people's lives. He has studied the Christian funeral and grieving process for twenty years. His 1980 book *The Death of A Christian: The Rite of Funerals* is a liturgical study of the rituals used in funeral services.